Our Leaders Speak

PRESIDENT DAVID O. McKAY

TYPICAL BRIGHAM YOUNG UNIVERSITY DEVOTIONAL ASSEMBLY

Our Leaders Speak

Eternal Truths
Spoken at Brigham Young University

COMPILED BY THE
BRIGHAM YOUNG UNIVERSITY
ADULT EDUCATION AND EXTENSION SERVICES
EXTENSION PUBLICATIONS

Selected and Arranged by
SOREN F. COX

DESERET BOOK COMPANY
Salt Lake City, Utah
1957

Second Printing

Printed by

in the United States of America

Acknowledgments

Many people participated in the compiling of this book. To acknowledge them all would be impossible, but I should like to extend appreciation to some, without whose assistance this book would not be: primarily to the General Authorities of the Church and other speakers at the Brigham Young University devotional assemblies who have been very generous in allowing the use of materials from their speeches; also to Brother Harold Glen Clark, Dean of Adult Education and Extension Services, Brigham Young University who suggested this book and supported it to completion; to Loree Brown and her staff of Extension Publications who worked tirelessly in assembling and typing the materials contained in this book; and to the Brigham Young University which sponsored the speakers in their appearances at devotional assemblies. To these and to all others who have assisted in this work, I express sincere thanks, with the hope that the worth of the book will justify their faith and efforts.

Soren F. Cox

Foreword

The Devotional Assembly at Brigham Young University is an hour of spiritual enlightenment when all regular studies and activities cease and the students gather at the George Albert Smith Fieldhouse to receive insight on the great verities of life. The speeches delivered by our leaders and other learned men and women during this devotional hour are filled with wisdom, spiritual uplift and sound advice. Because of the wealth of material found in these addresses, Brigham Young University through its Adult Education and Extension Services, has sponsored the compilation of selected portions of each speech.

In *Our Leaders Speak*, Soren F. Cox of the Brigham Young University English Department has made a careful designation of choice excerpts taken from the full text of each speech and arranged them in ready reference form. Mr. Cox, as a successful teacher of English and as an experienced officer in church and civic life, has lifted from the text, those stories and quotations which bear directly upon the daily lives of men and women both young and old.

The central aim of the Extension Services of the Brigham Young University is to help us change ourselves in desirable ways. *Our Leaders Speak* was compiled to give wider circulation to the knowledge, values, testimonies and concepts given to us by our leaders. We hope that students, parents and teachers, and others in church and civic life will find this source book especially useful and inspiring.

HAROLD GLEN CLARK, Dean
Adult Education and Extension Services

Contents

	PAGE
THE ATONEMENT	1
CHARACTER	3
CITIZENSHIP	8
COURTSHIP AND MARRIAGE	14
DEATH AND RESURRECTION	29
DEATH	30
EDUCATION	32
ETERNAL LIFE	47
FAITH	49
FREE AGENCY	55
FREEDOM	60
GAMBLING	65
GODHEAD	66
GOVERNMENT	68
GRATITUDE	72
HOME AND FAMILY	74
HONESTY	81
JESUS CHRIST	82
JOSEPH SMITH	88
JOY	95
LAW	96
LIVING OUR RELIGION	97
MISSIONARY WORK	111
MORALS	115
OBEDIENCE	117
PATRIARCHAL BLESSINGS	121
PIONEERS	122
PRACTICAL RELIGION	125

PAGE

PRAYER 126
PRE-EXISTENCE 135
PRIESTHOOD 137
REPENTANCE 143
REVELATION 149
SACRAMENT 155
SERVICE 157
SPIRITUAL GIFTS 158
TEMPLE WORK 166
TESTIMONY 168
TITHING 175
TRUTH 176
UNITED ORDER 183
WISDOM 184
WORD OF WISDOM 186
WORK 193

Sources

The quotations contained in this book have been selected from speeches presented to the Brigham Young University studentbody in its weekly devotional assembly. The name and the number following each quotation indicate the speaker and the source from which the excerpt was taken.

The position listed after the speaker indicates the position held at the time the speech was given.

The full text of each speech is available in mimeograph form for a nominal fee from the Brigham Young University Extension Publications, Provo, Utah.

MARK K. ALLEN, Acting Chairman, Department of Psychology, Brigham Young University.
The Mature Personality at Work 12-8-52

ARCHIBALD F. BENNETT, Secretary, Genealogical Society
The Joy of Temple Building and Temple Service 3-6-56

ADAM S. BENNION, Council of the Twelve Apostles
1. The "Y" in Y-O-U 3-29-55
2. The Upward Reach 1-31-56

LOWELL L. BENNION, Director, LDS Institute of Religion, University of Utah
Practical Mormonism 11-5-52

EZRA TAFT BENSON, Council of the Twelve Apostles
1. LDS Church and Politics 12-1-52
2. Responsibilities of Citizenship 10-22-54
3. Baccalaureate Sermon 6-2-55

WILLIAM E. BERRETT, Vice President, Religious Education, Brigham Young University
The Road to Freedom 1-12-54

HUGH B. BROWN, Assistant to the Council of the Twelve Apostles
1. Why Religious Education 2-16-54
2. Personal Liberty vs. Social Control 11-9-54
3. The Profile of a Prophet 10-4-55
4. Baccalaureate Sermon 5-31-56
5. Search For God 11-13-56

CARL W. BUEHNER, Second Counselor, Presiding Bishopric
Our "Corporate" Opportunities and Responsibilities 1-8-57

PARLEY A. CHRISTENSEN, English Department, Brigham Young
University
The Unearned Goodness 11-20-56

ELRAY L. CHRISTIANSEN, Assistant to the Council of the Twelve
Apostles
1. Temple Marriage 2-4-53
2. The Fullness of Joy Comes through Obedience to Law
12-4-56

BRUCE B. CLARK, English Department, Brigham Young University
Karl G. Maeser Anniversary 10-25-55

J. REUBEN CLARK, Jr., Second Counselor in the First Presidency
1. Who Was This Jesus? 12-11-51
2. A Simple Faith 5-13-53
3. The World Is Waiting to Test You 4-20-54
4. As Ye Sow . . . 5-3-55
5. Jesus the Christ—Creator and Redeemer 5-22-56
6. Our Political Blessings 5-21-57

MATTHEW COWLEY, Council of the Twelve Apostles
1. Miracles 2-18-53
2. Achievement 5-18-53
3. Put Your Hand into the Hand of God 10-20-53

ELBERT R. CURTIS, General Superintendent, YMMIA
Why an All-Church Basketball Tournament 3-4-54

GERRIT deJONG, Jr., Dean, College of Fine Arts, Brigham Young
University
Art and Life 1-5-53

CECIL B. DeMILLE, Movie Producer, Paramount Studios
Commencement Address 6-1-57

HENRY ALDOUS DIXON, President, Utah State Agricultural
College
The College Assembly Period and Christian Living 3-23-54

WILLIAM F. EDWARDS, Vice President, Finance, Brigham Young
University
From Each According to His Ability, To Each According to His
Need 4-13-54

RICHARD L. EVANS, Council of the Twelve Apostles
  1. The Spirit that Leads to Truth 12-1-53
  2. Beginnings 2-14-56
  3. Be the Best You Know How 2-12-57

LAVINA FUGAL, American Mother of the Year—1955
  "Love Never Faileth" 4-24-56

EARL J. GLADE, Mayor, Salt Lake City, Utah
  Your Good Name 5-11-53

MARION D. HANKS, First Council of the Seventy
  1. What Is True Freedom? 2-9-54
  2. Through the Eyes and Mouths of Children 1-10-56
  3. Baccalaureate Sermon 8-16-56
  4. Seeking "Thick" Things 3-26-57

SPENCER W. KIMBALL, Council of the Twelve Apostles
  1. Be Ye Clean 5-4-54
  2. Tragedy or Destiny? 12-6-55

DAVID S. KING, Second Assistant General Superintendent, YMMIA
  The Glory of Participation 3-28-57

OSCAR A. KIRKHAM, First Council of Seventy
  In Us You Live Again 11-19-52

HAROLD B. LEE, Council of the Twelve Apostles
  1. Divine Revelation 10-15-52
  2. Cram For Life's Final Examination 1-5-54
  3. "By Their Fruits Ye Shall Know Them" 10-12-54
  4. Feet Shod with the Preparation of the Gospel of Peace 11-9-54
  5. "But Arise and Stand Upon Thy Feet"—And I Will Speak
     with Thee 2-7-56
  6. "Eye Hath Not Seen . . ." 10-2-56

JOHN LONGDEN, Assistant to the Council of the Twelve Apostles
  A Latter-day Saint—Always a Missionary 4-30-57

BRUCE R. McCONKIE, First Council of the Seventy
  1. The Atonement 5-6-53
  2. Celestial Marriage 11-15-55
  3. Keys of the Kingdom 4-23-57

DAVID O. McKAY, President, Church of Jesus Christ of Latter-day
  Saints
  1. Message for LDS Youth 10-8-52
  2. Dedicatory Address and Prayer 5-26-54

3. Five Ideals Contributive to a Happy Marriage 10-11-55
4. Gospel Ideals—Life's Surest Anchor 10-30-56

THOMAS E. McKAY, Assistant to the Council of the Twelve Apostles
Standards for LDS Youth 1-19-53

LYNN A. McKINLAY, Speech Department, Brigham Young
University
Giving Thanks 11-22-55

WENDELL MENDENHALL, President, San Joaquin Stake, California
Remember the Worth of Souls Is Great in the Sight of God
1-26-54

NICHOLAS G. MORGAN, Sr., President, Sons of Utah Pioneers
Our Heritage 10-27-53

GEORGE Q. MORRIS, Council of the Twelve Apostles
1. The Importance of Habits 5-20-53
2. Church Doctrines 1-11-55
3. Truth and Power of God 2-19-57

HENRY D. MOYLE, Council of the Twelve Apostles
1. Views on U. S. Government Policy 10-22-52
2. Unto Every Kingdom a Law Is Given 10-13-53
2. Unity Under the Gospel 3-22-55
4. Personality of God 1-24-56
5. Education—A Commitment to Responsibility 1-29-57

JAY B. NASH, Dean, College of Recreation, Physical and Health
Education, and Athletics, Brigham Young University
They Never Had a Chance 5-15-56

PRESTON NIBLEY, Assistant Church Historian
The Manuscripts of the Book of Mormon 4-9-57

HENRY J. NICHOLES, Zoology Department, Brigham Young
University
Science, Religion, and Diet 1-12-53

MARK E. PETERSEN, Council of the Twelve Apostles
1. Tolerance 4-29-53
2. Chastity 2-3-53
3. Stability 3-9-54
4. We Believe in Being True 10-5-54
5. We Believe in Being Honest 11-1-55
6. Live For Our Faith 10-16-56

ROSE MARIE REID, Designer and Executive
How the Gospel Influenced My Life 6-1-53

LeGRAND RICHARDS, Council of the Twelve Apostles
1. Patriarchal Blessings 5-27-53
2. Preparation for Marriage 3-3-54
3. Prophecy 3-16-54
4. A Testimony 5-10-55
5. A Choice Seer and Prophet Like Unto Moses 3-27-56

STEPHEN L RICHARDS, First Counselor in the First Presidency
1. Missionary Work 1-19-54
2. David O. McKay Building Dedication 12-14-54
3. Double Taxation for BYU—Does It Pay? 2-28-56
4. Counsel 2-26-57

MARION G. ROMNEY, Council of the Twelve Apostles
1. How to Gain a Testimony 3-25-53
2. The Perfect Law of Liberty 3-30-54
3. The Price of Peace 3-1-55
4. ". . . Ye Are a Peculiar People" 4-10-56
5. A Practical Religion 1-15-57
6. Your Quest For Truth 5-30-57

STERLING W. SILL, Assistant to the Council of the Twelve Apostles
1. The Miracle of Personality 4-13-53
2. Vision 9-25-54
3. An Inside Job 3-15-55

GEORGE ALBERT SMITH, Jr., Business Administration, Harvard University
Some Challenges for LDS Students 11-8-55

JOSEPH FIELDING SMITH, President, Council of the Twelve Apostles
1. The Atonement of Jesus Christ 1-25-55
2. The Purpose of Mortal Life 5-1-56
3. "For Ye Are Bought with a Price . . ." 5-14-57

MILAN D. SMITH, President of Union Stake, Oregon
Meeting the World and Maintaining Your Church Standards 11-2-53

RAY F. SMITH, LDS Chaplain, Utah State Prison
Prison Work—You Can't Judge a Man by His Record 2-5-57

ALMA SONNE, Assistant to the Council of the Twelve Apostles
The Bedrock of Spirituality 2-25-53

BELLE S. SPAFFORD, General President, Relief Society
International Women 3-8-55

DELBERT L. STAPLEY, Council of the Twelve Apostles
1. Revealed Truth—Basis of Wisdom 5-11-54
2. The Sacrament 5-8-56

A. WALTER STEVENSON, First Assistant General Superintendent,
YMMIA
Why an All Church Basketball Tournament 3-4-54

NELDON E. TANNER, President Calgary Stake, Canada
Commencement Address 6-1-56

HARVEY L. TAYLOR, Executive Assistant to President, Brigham
Young University
This Is Our Country, 11-10-53

ERNEST L. WILKINSON, President, Brigham Young University
1. Charge to Graduates 6-1-56
2. The Trial of Jesus 4-1-53

JOSEPH L. WIRTHLIN, Presiding Bishop
The Powers and Prerogatives of the Aaronic Priesthood 5-18-54

S. DILWORTH YOUNG, First Council of the Seventy
Personal Prayer 1-28-53

The *Atonement*

Importance of the Atonement. The atonement is the most transcendent doctrine of the gospel. It is the most important single thing that has ever occurred in the history of the world, or ever will occur. It is the foundation upon which all other things rest. If it weren't for the atonement, we could write the gospel off as a myth and the whole purpose of the creation would be frustrated. [*Bruce R. McConkie* 1]

The Savior and the Atonement. Now, the atoning sacrifice of Jesus Christ was worked out in the Garden of Gethsemane, primarily. It was culminated or ended on the cross, but it was in the Garden where the great suffering took place, where he sweat, as it were, great drops of blood from every pore, and where he took upon himself our sins on condition of repentance. [*Bruce R. McConkie* 1]

Understanding the Atonement. Now in order to understand, insofar as we can, the doctrine of the atonement of Christ, it is necessary for us to accept and believe two fundamental truths. We must believe, first, in the divine Sonship of Jesus Christ. We must believe that he is literally the Son of God, as you and I are the sons of our mortal parents, because, except for that kind of birth, he would not have had power to bring to pass the resurrection of all men and offer all men eternal life on condition of obedience. The second truth that we must accept and believe is that God created Adam and that Adam fell, bringing into the world, first, a spiritual death and secondly, a temporal death.

Now there isn't anything in the world, and there isn't anything in eternity, that in any way can compare in importance with the atoning sacrifice of Jesus Christ. We don't understand all things about it. But what has been revealed, we are in duty bound to accept and understand, and we are in duty bound—if we value our souls and desire an inheritance in the eternal kingdom of the Father—we are in duty bound to conform our lives to those principles which will make the atonement efficacious for us as far as its spiritual side is concerned. It is automatically efficacious for us in the temporal sense. [*Bruce R. McConkie* 1]

Character

Character in the Gospel. The greatest force in the world for us is making habits of principles and the building of character in the gospel of Jesus Christ. [*George Q. Morris* 1]

Possibilities for Character Development. I would like to give it as my opinion that the greatest waste there is in the world is not the devastation that goes with war; nor is it the burden of expense that follows crime; nor is it both of these put together. The greatest waste there is in the world is that people—you and I—live so far below the level of our possibilities. [*Sterling W. Sill* 3]

. . . The greatest values in the world are those great potentialities within ourselves. The most profitable thing that any one of us can do . . . is to develop those qualities that too often lie undiscovered and undeveloped in human beings. [*Sterling W. Sill* 1]

Influence of Thought on Character. Thoughts are the tools with which we shape our character, just as truly as a great sculptor with chisel and mallet chips and chips on the rough marble until it is shaped, perhaps, into a Moses, or a David—a splendid and perfect work of art. Just so every thought is shaping our character and consequently, shaping our destiny and our lives. [*George Q. Morris* 1]

There is a story about a peculiar custom of a group of ancient Chinese. If you visited in one of their homes and admired a certain object, you might find that your Chinese host would wrap this particular article up and send it to you as a present. You admire it and so you get it. But that is exactly what life does to us all of the time. Whatever you truly love and admire, you get. If you love honesty, you get honesty. If you love friendship, you get friendship. If you love integrity or industry, or any other trait, good or bad, life wraps it up and sends it to you as a present. [*Sterling W. Sill* 1]

Depth of Character.   There is a far greater percentage of people who know what is right than there is who do what is right. There are a hundred men who believe in honesty for every honest man. There are a hundred men who believe in religion for every truly religious man. Mostly we live too much on the surface; whereas character goes deeper. The reason so many of us fail in life is because we take only that part of the mind into our work with us which we call the conscious mind. We never learn how to use that great creative power called the subconscious mind which God has made a part of every human soul. When we do use this part of our mind, we sometimes use it as a dumping ground for doubt, fear, hate, lethargy, indecision, guilt complexes, inferiority complexes and sin. [*Sterling W. Sill* 3]

Breadth of Character.   The mature person is one whose self extends far beyond the limits of his own body. The mature self is one who takes genuinely into account other people and their welfare. The concept of this need to extend the self is a very broad one. Instrumental to satisfying this core need are other sorts of social needs which are often very significant in our lives. They are: first, the need for achievement; second, the need for belonging; third, the need for social approval, through which we get the image of ourselves, in terms of which we conceive what manner of person we are; fourth, the need for affection; and fifth, the need for independence. [*Mark K. Allen*]

Principle and Character.   No one is great for himself alone. He is great because of what he believes in and stands for and fights for. Lincoln was great because of what he stood for; Joseph Smith was great because of what he stood for. The most humble of us can stand for the greatest things. Neither are we great for what we are, but we are great for what we may become. And we will become tomorrow what we stand for today. [*Sterling W. Sill 3*]

I am sure that it is the desire of each of you to lead a full, rich life. You will find it necessary frequently to stand alone rather than to go down the easier path with the multitude. There is no victory in surrendering to temptations. Nothing of great worth comes the easy way. Your character is continually being molded. If it is above reproach, you will leave a noble contribution for the benefit of your posterity. [*Milan D. Smith*]

Character Despite Adversity. Money is, of course, very necessary; it is a necessary evil. I wish I had more of it. But I would rather know how to live and have ideas and ideals to live to, than acquire wealth, because I know that when I come to die it doesn't matter how much money others have, they will not take with them any more than I will.

Achievement. It's a wonderful thing. I think now of Michael J. Dowling, a young man who fell from a wagon in a blizzard in Michigan when he was fourteen years of age. Before his parents discovered that he had fallen from the rear of the wagon, he had been frostbitten. His right leg was amputated almost to the hip, his left leg above the knee; his right arm was amputated, his left hand was amputated. Not much future for a young lad like that, was there? Do you know what he did? He went to the board of county commissioners and he told them that if they would educate him he would pay them back every penny.

During the First World War, Mr. Dowling, who was at the time president of one of the largest banks in St. Paul, went to Europe to visit the soldiers—to visit those who were wounded. I remember reading that upon one occasion he was in a large hotel in London, and he had before him the wounded soldiers in their wheel chairs. They were in the lobby and he was up on the mezzanine floor. As he started to speak he minimized the seriousness of their wounds; the fact that one had lost an eye, another had lost an arm, etc., was no grounds for complaint. And he got those fellows so wrought up that they started to boo him. Then he walked over to the stairway and down the stairs toward the lobby, telling them as he walked how fortunate they were, and they continued booing. Finally, he sat down on one of the steps and took off his right leg. And he kept on talking, and telling them how well off they were. Well, they calmed down a little bit, but still they resented his remarks. Then he took off his left leg. Well, the booing stopped then. But before he arrived at the bottom of the stairs, he had taken off his right arm and flipped off his left hand, and there he sat—just the stump of a body!

Michael Dowling was the president of one of the biggest banks in St. Paul. He had married, and was the father of five children. . . . He knew how to live, and he knew how to make money, and he knew how to rear a family—and he finally died as the result of the strength he gave in encouraging the wounded soldiers of the First World War. [*Matthew Cowley* 2]

Dare to Do.   When I was a small boy, quite small, a group of us had a swimming hole. We spent quite a bit of time down there—too much, so my mother thought. We couldn't wait until the snow was off in the spring to get down to the swimming hole. I remember going down there one afternoon after school was out—instead of hurrying home as we were expected to, we went down to the swimming hole. The snow was off on the south bank, but there was snow and ice under the willows on the north bank. The grass looked warm and dry. So we stripped off, and while the grass was dry, the ground was damp and cold. I dipped my toes in the water, then my fingers, and stepped back on the bank shivering. Two or three of the others did the same thing. We each decided that it was too cold. We dressed and went out. There was one in that group, however, that didn't put his fingers nor his toes in; he just ducked under. He said, "Come on in, boys; the water's fine." He enjoyed the swim. He's President of the Church today. [*Thomas E. McKay*]

Citizenship

Individual Responsibility for Citizenship. This remember well: you can serve your country best if you put on the whole armor of God. Then you will be blessed with muscles and nerves of iron and a keen mind to help you understand and resolve the multiplicity of conflicting events which go to make up your daily life. Try to remember that ancient civilizations, one after another, fell and crumbled into decay because their citizens became weak in spirit, body, mind, and national honor. [*Harvey L. Taylor*]

Principle and Citizenship. There is, my fellow Americans, a Force in the universe which no mortal can alter. We must make certain that our policies and our programs conform with those eternal principles which have been set forth by that Force, by the God of Heaven. In other words, we need to raise our sights beyond the dollar sign, beyond material things. We need to recognize that America has become a great nation because she has adhered wholeheartedly to certain basic Christian principles that are eternal. We must have an adherence to these high moral principles, these spiritual principles, if this nation is to endure. God grant that it may endure! [*Ezra Taft Benson 2*]

Elder Ezra Taft Benson's Call to Become Secretary of Agriculture. Now I presume, my brothers and sisters, that you'll be disappointed . . . if I don't tell you something of the rather intimate situation in connection with this call [Secretary of Agriculture]. And if I can, in just a few words, I'd like to do it for you because I feel so close to this institution [BYU]. I hope you'll understand that it isn't done in any spirit of boasting, but in the hope it may be helpful. Since the call has come, I have felt more like praying than anything else. Of course, I've done a great deal of it, and I hope I'll have your faith and prayers, because this honor is not an honor only to an individual member of the Church. I look upon it as an honor and a tribute to the Church as a whole. It is an evidence that, at last, people have come to recognize us for what we are—to recognize our standards, our ideals, our philosophy, the principles for which we stand. And so you share in this honor, and you also share in the responsibility, and to that end I seek your faith and prayers in the days ahead.

Now it has come as a great surprise. It is true that four years ago [1948] I was approached regarding a cabinet post by one of the candidates . . . but frankly this time [1952] the matter had never entered my head. Senator Watkins, in a telephone call on Thursday night, the 20th of November, asked if I knew that there was developing a great "ground-swell," as he called it, of support for me as Secretary. This was my first intimation that I was being considered. I said no, I knew nothing about it. And I was truthful. Brother Watkins wanted to know what the attitude of the Church would be. I replied, "There's only one man who can answer that, and that's the President of the Church. I don't know what his attitude would be. My life is devoted to the work of the Church, but I'd be glad to try and do anything the President of the Church asks me to do."

The next morning as I parked my car on the parking lot at the Church Office Building, I met President David O. McKay as he was parking his car. . . . And he said, "I received a very important telephone call last night. Brother Benson, my mind is clear in the matter and if the opportunity comes, I think you should accept."

I said, "Brother McKay, I can't believe that it will come," and gave my reasons. The next day Brother Mark

E. Petersen and I started for Provo to attend to some business incident to the division of the Sharon Stake. On arrival in Provo the call from Eisenhower Headquarters in New York City came and reached me in this city, Provo. When I learned of it, the first place I thought of was the campus of the BYU where I could get to myself in some little office and quietly consider the matter. I talked to the President of the Church by telephone before I even accepted the New York telephone call, because they said that General Eisenhower's office was calling. The call was simply a request to come to New York City for an interview, and frankly, even then, I thought that probably they were considering several men and they wanted a chance to look at some of them with whom they were not acquainted. I took the plane that night and went to New York City for the interview.

I can say to you frankly, my brothers and sisters, I didn't want to be Secretary of Agriculture. I can't imagine anyone in his right mind wanting the position. Because I know something of what it entails; I know something of the crossfires, the pressures, the problems, the difficulties. Because as Brother Wilkinson has been good enough to indicate, I was rather close to the Department of Agriculture, although not a part of it, while living for five and a half years in Washington. I've always feared, in a way, getting into politics. I've never had any particular desire in that direction. I've always had a deep interest in seeing men elected to office who represented the ideals and standards which have meant so much to me in my life, but I would always rather support someone else than to actually hold political office.

It was with that feeling in mind that I went to meet, for the first time, General Eisenhower. I'm sure that he would not object if I told you very briefly what transpired. His brother, Milton Eisenhower, whom I had met, was there. He at one time was in the Department of Agriculture; he at one time was president of Kansas State College, and now [1952] is president of Pennsylvania State College, both of them land-grant colleges. The President-elect and I were together for about thirty minutes, and at the outset it was made very clear that the decision had been made. There was no one else under consideration. Then I gave him three or four very good reasons, I thought, why I should not be a member of the Cabinet. In the first place I indicated that I had been a supporter of Senator Robert A. Taft. Although not an active supporter, I had lent my name to a Citizens for Taft Committee. I thought Senator Taft was well qualified; I'd known him in Washington and admired his integrity and capacity. And I said to the General, "It isn't because I haven't admired you, but I haven't known you; I've never seen you until today. And I've always thought it would be a little better, other things being equal, not to have a military man in the White House. Now I want you to know that."

He said, "That's perfectly all right."

I said for my next reason, "I come from a state that is usually considered rather unimportant agriculturally. Even my native state of Idaho is not one of the leading agricultural states. It has been the custom to select the Secretary of Agriculture from the great farm belt of the Middle West. What's going to be the reaction if you select as your Secretary of Agriculture a man from Utah where only three percent of our land area is under cultivation? I know there are several good men in the Middle West who would like to be Secretary. And at least three of them I could wholeheartedly support; they'd make good secretaries, and they've been working hard for you and surely you owe them something." And fourthly I said, "I wonder about the wisdom of calling a clergyman, a minister of the gospel, to be a Secretary of Agriculture. What will be the reaction from other religious groups, and from people generally?"

And he said, "Suppose we consider the last question first." Then he added, "Surely you believe that the job to be done is spiritual. Surely you know that we have the great responsibility to restore confidence in the minds of our people in their own government—that we've got to deal with spiritual matters." Then he went on and answered the rest of my objections. When he came to the end he said, "We've got a great job to do. I didn't want to be President, frankly, when the pressure started." But he said, *"You can't refuse to serve America!* We've got a great job to do and I want you on my team."

Well, my brothers and sisters, no true American could refuse such a request from the President-elect, even though I told him I had already received, what in my eyes was a greater honor than he could bestow. So, of course, I accepted. [*Ezra Taft Benson* 1]

Obligation of Church Members to Serve in Service Organizations. When I was named President of Relief Society, one of the first invitations to reach my desk was one to attend a biennial meeting of the National Council of Women. This was at a time following the war, when the Council was at a low ebb and when, at least in my opinion, I felt that Mormon women were not being properly considered. Gathering up a number of arguments as ammunition, I went to President George Albert Smith with the recommendation that Relief Society withdraw from the Council. I concluded my argument in favor of my position by saying, "Relief Society is really getting nothing from the Council."

In his characteristic manner, President Smith leaned back on his chair and smiled. Then he said, "Sister Spafford, you surprise me a little. Do you always think in terms of what you get? Don't you ever think in terms of what you have to give? Mormon women have something to give to the women of the world. You had better retain your membership and accept this invitation. Take Sister Priscilla Evans, a member of your board and an attorney and other board members, and give something to the women of your nation and to the women of the world."

. . . Needless to say we attended the New York Council with pronounced feelings of obligation and with a full determination to make a contribution to the work of the Council. This has been our determination since that time. [*Belle S. Spafford*]

Courtship and Marriage

Conduct on Dates. Recently Sister McKay read to me a letter written by a young girl in her teens. Without giving any names, I am going to quote from that letter as illustrative of one of the topics that I am going to name this morning as contributing to a happy marriage, the first of which is *maintaining a good reputation*. A happy marriage begins before you go to the altar. It begins while you are accepting invitations in your teen-age years to go to parties. It begins with the manner in which you say good night to your companions.

This girl writes:

Being a teen-ager is quite confusing to me because there are so many temptations and problems which seem to come all at once. One of these problems which has bothered me a great deal concerns dating. I have heard so many different ideas and explanations on this subject that I am quite confused.

But I have gone out with boys for a good year and a half, and I have learned many things. I have felt that I would like to save my affection until I meet the man that I am to marry. However, several of my friends seriously disagree with me and feel that I am being an extremist. They have made me very unhappy because of many things they have said, and I have begun to wonder if some of my ideas might be wrong.

Most all of us agree that it is wrong to sit and kiss and spoon for long periods of time. I am completely against that, but they tell me that after a boy has taken me out several times and shown me a good time, I should show my appreciation by a good night kiss. I have never felt this to be true, and several boys that I have dated have been quite offended, and feeling that I did not like them, they have quit asking me out. When I do finally meet the man I should marry, I shall want to give him all my love and affection, and I believe that the kiss will mean more if it has not been thrown to all the other boys, too.

She was in doubt as to what she should do, and she wrote to one who she thought could help her. I should like to present to all the young people of the Church, through you, a safe guide in regard to your actions, young ladies, towards young men; and to you young men a guide for your actions towards young women. . . .

That young girl could be safely guided, as every young girl, if she stops to say, "What will my actions tonight do to my mother, and my father, to the standards of purity in our home?" That is a safe guide for our actions in life regarding our own eternal parents. [*David O. McKay* 3]

Single Standard of Morality. If you would have a happy marriage, keep your reputation unsullied. I remember as a boy, in my teens, a summer afternoon walk with sweet companions. We walked up the "middle lane" leading to South Fork Canyon. On each side of the road were wild roses. We did not stop to pluck any because they were covered with the dust of travelers. We soon reached the hillside. There, too, were roses, free from the dust of the traveler, each one kissed only by the sunshine and the morning dew. We plucked the unsullied rose and gave to the girl companion who seemed so worthy of it.

This principle seems to me to strike right at the base of happiness in the marriage relations—a standard of purity taught and practiced among the Latter-day Saints. It is a common saying throughout the world that young men may sow their wild oats, but young women should be chaperoned and guarded; and be it said to their credit, that generally young women are protected. The young men, however, are given too free license, if statistics tell the truth. In the Church of Christ there is but one standard of morality. No young man has any more right to sow his wild oats in youth than has a young girl; and she is taught that second only to the crime of taking human life is that of losing her virtue, and that should be the ideal among young men.

* * *

No one can transgress the laws of chastity and find peace. That is the message to our boys and girls . . . throughout the Church. No matter what the opportunity, no matter what the temptation, let the young man know that to find happiness, he must hold sacred his true manhood. Let him know that he is going to live and live completely by refusing to yield to the temptations. Then he is happy. There is peace instead of turbulency in his soul. [*David O. McKay* 3]

Dangers of Petting. This is a true story. The characters are real.

It was a long-distance call; that was quite apparent, for as I picked up the receiver I could hear the coins dropping in a faraway coin box, then a voice asking, "Brother Kimball?"

I answered, "Yes."

It was a young man's voice saying, "I have a very personal problem. Could I bring my girl friend and come to see you?"

"Of course," I said, and a time was arranged.

It was not long until the young couple was announced. The deep pleasant voice was just what one might expect from the tall, athletic youth who possessed it. He was well proportioned, and like King David, "ruddy and withal of a beautiful countenance and goodly to look at." (1 Samuel 16:12.)

With him was a lovely girl, slight of frame and beautiful of face and form. They were both dressed well, and it was evident that they were from cultured homes. It was also obvious that they loved each other, for as they sat together across the desk from me he reached quietly for her hand.

The melodious voice was hesitant and a bit choked with emotion as he introduced his girl friend, and there was pleading in their eyes. "We are in difficulty, Brother Kimball," he said, "we have broken the law of chastity. We have defiled ourselves. We prayed and fasted and agonized and finally came to the conclusion that we must try to make adjustments."

I asked them a few questions. It was evident they had been treading deep waters. The girl took over the conversation, "I had convinced myself that I was able to take care of myself, that I would never commit this abhorrent sin. I have heard the brethren say repeatedly that necking and petting were sins in their own right, but I would not let myself believe it."

I let them tell the story without interruption, feeling it would enable them to unload the heavy burden they were carrying.

The boy was now speaking. He was self-accusing. "That Junior Prom date was a very special one," he continued. "But it turned out to be a tragic one, the beginning of sorrows. When I saw my sweetheart coming downstairs that night, I thought no girl was ever so beautiful and so sweet. We danced through the evening; and then when we sat in the car, long and silently afterward, my thoughts became unruly as we made love. Neither of us dreamed of what was happening to us," he said, "but all the elements were there to break down resistance. We did not notice time—the hours passed. Our usual elementary necking gradually developed into petting. There were other nights —the bars were down. We loved each other so much that we convinced ourselves that it was not so wrong since we sort of belonged to each other anyway. Where we ended the other night became the starting point this night, and we continued on and on, and finally it happened—the terrible thing happened. We had vowed it would never envelop us. And then when it was late—so late—so everlastingly late, we awoke to our plight. We hated ourselves. We mentally thrashed ourselves. She suggested we pray, but I told her

I felt too unworthy. I wanted to hide from the Lord, from everybody. Oh, Brother Kimball, what can we do? Is it unpardonable? Are we lost forever? Can we ever gain forgiveness?"

His voice broke and there was a heavy silence.

I sat down in thought praying fervently that the Lord would inspire me to assist them.

They seemed to want to talk. It was as though a great flood of feelings needed release.

"I am so ashamed," she said. "I was not guiltless. When we reached home, he turned off the engine. We became quiet; the conversation lagged; and the thing began to happen against which we had been warned and rewarned. The goodnight kiss was a warm, passionate, long-sustained one, and we lingered longer. When I knelt at my bed that night I asked the Lord to forgive me, and I think (at that moment) I honestly intended never to repeat the process."

"I felt I loved him as no girl ever loved one before. He was good, but he was human. The necking evolved into petting sooner each night, and a new pattern was being established. I felt guilty when I went in. I didn't feel much like praying. Why should I? What use to pray when I would likely continue. I wasn't so sure I wanted to quit. It wasn't so bad anyway, was it? We hadn't committed fornication and wouldn't—certainly we wouldn't. That we knew."

"Little did we realize that each time there were new excesses. And suddenly we awakened to the fact that we had lost our virtue totally—had lost that most priceless thing—we had committed that most abominable sin. I loathed myself. Why had I not listened? Why had I disregarded counsel? Why had I not run, screamed, fought, died? There was no sleep for me this night. I was unclean. I bathed, scrubbed, washed my hair, put on fresh clothes. I was still filthy. I remembered the lepers in Bible days—how they stood afar off and cried to an approaching person, 'unclean, unclean.' I felt like a leper, like hiding, like avoiding everyone. My soul cried out in agony. Could I keep others from hearing the sobbing of my heart?

"In the sleepless nights were horrible dreams, nightmares. Why must I be so plagued? Other young people had done this terrible thing. It did not seem to wreck them. They seemed to pass it off with a shrug of the shoulders, but I—

"Hell? Yes, this is hell. We always thought of hell as a faraway, mythical and abstract thing, but we've found it—we've tasted it—it is bitter, very bitter. Why weren't youth warned of these horrors? Then I remembered we had been warned, all our lives. Why had we not listened? Why did we remain in the car late at night after we should have said goodnight?"

She could not stop. It was like the flood of the waters escaping from a broken reservoir. "A thousand thoughts ran through my mind," she said, "ugly accusing thoughts— when I ate, when I walked, when I prayed. The ghost memory taunted me."

And now they sat very still, very close, waiting, almost breathlessly. "Children of disobedience," I thought. My heart was sobbing for them; "Please, Father, bless me that I may help them."

"Can we ever be forgiven, Brother Kimball," they asked plaintively.

"Yes, beloved youth," I replied, "the Lord and his Church can forgive, but not easily. 'The way of the transgressor is hard.' It ever has been—it always will be. The Lord himself said:

I tell thee thou shalt not depart thence till thou hast paid the very last mite. (Luke 12:59.)

But, in his goodness, he provided for us a way to forgiveness. One may do as he pleases, but he cannot evade responsibility. He may break laws, but he cannot avoid penalties. One gets by with nothing. No one ever gets anything for nothing. God is just.

Be not deceived, [said Paul,] God is not mocked, for whatsoever a man soweth, that shall he also reap. (Galatians 6:7.)

Again:

Mortify therefore your members which are upon the earth; fornication, uncleanness, inordinate affection, evil concupiscence and covetousness, . . . for which things' sake, the wrath of God cometh on the children of disobedience. (Colossians 3:5-6.)

Serious as are these abominable things, there is forgiveness conditioned upon total repentance. The Prophet Amulek quoted the Lord:

. . . and he hath said that no unclean thing can inherit the kingdom of heaven; therefore, how can ye be saved except ye inherit the kingdom of heaven? Therefore, ye cannot be saved in your sins. (Alma 11:37.)

And Isaiah:

. . . Let the wicked forsake his way . . . and let him return unto the Lord, . . . for he will abundantly pardon. (Isaiah 55:6-7.)

Yes, the Lord will forgive. How *grateful* we must be for this saving principle!

Behold, he who has repented of his sins, the same is forgiven, and I the Lord remember them no more. (Doctrine & Covenants 58:42.)

How *glorious* this promise!

. . . though your sins be as scarlet, they shall be as white as snow; though they be red like crimson, they shall be as wool. (Isaiah 1:18.)
[*Spencer W. Kimball* 1]

[Read the entire address. Elder Kimball has pointed out in the balance of the address not only that forgiveness is possible, but some of the steps necessary to obtain that adjustment.]

Eternal Courtship. Too many couples look upon the covenant at the marriage altar as the end of courtship. It should be the beginning of an eternal courtship. . . . [*David O. McKay* 3]

Celestial Marriage. Young men, I'd like to ask you this question. Do you not think that it would be disappointing to any girl in this Church who understands these things [principles of celestial marriage] to make a proposal to her for a marriage less enduring, less significant, than temple marriage? If a man were to go to a girl in the Christian world, having their concept of marriage, and say, "My dear, I would like you to marry me, but I only want you for a few years. I don't want you for all your life." Of course, that girl would be affronted by such a proposal. Ought not the girl of this Church be likewise disappointed and affronted with a proposal for marriage which says in substance, "I'm willing to take you for the short period of our natural lives, but I don't want you hereafter." Isn't that in substance what a young man of the Church says to a young woman of the Church when he proposes marriage that is not of the highest order?" [*Stephen L Richards* 1]

Living Worthy for Celestial Marriage. A few years ago I was invited to the Beehive House to meet with a group of girls who had been shepherded there in a club during the war years to try to keep them from falling into evil ways while they were away from their homes, from country towns for the most part. After I had fulfilled my assignment and was about to leave, a young girl drew me aside and asked if she could speak to me a moment. She opened her purse and took out of it a picture of a handsome young soldier in uniform and underneath it said something about love, and was signed by this man. Then she took out from behind the picture a folded piece of paper and as she was doing this tears were swimming in her eyes, and I said, "Well, what does this all mean?"

She said, "Brother Lee, I met this young man out here in one of the camps. He was a fine young man, clean, good habits, always treated me with respect, gentlemanly. I felt perfectly safe when I was out on a date with him, all but for one thing: he was not a member of the Church. Finally he proposed marriage and I said, 'Well, I love you, Jack, but we have got to think about something else. Marriage to us is more than just something for this life. If it is the genuine kind of love, it should last always and should make us husband and wife forever.' Well, at first he argued with me, then he became angry and then he was out of patience and finally the time came when he had his overseas orders to go into combat area and this time he pressed the matter of our engagement and I said to him plainly, 'No, I can't marry anywhere until I can be married in the House of the Lord.'"

And he had replied in anger, "All right, if you think more of your Church and your religion than you do of me, why you can have them but you can't have me."

I guess she cried herself to sleep or cried all night without sleep, I don't know which. But when he got on the boat, there were some two or three weeks before he arrived at his destination down in Australia which was to be the staging area for the fights up in the Islands, and on the way over he had time to think about all she had said to him . . . this sweet, lovely girl that to him represented the ideal of his life. She was everything that he could ask for in a sweetheart, his wife, the mother of his children. Then he started thinking, "I wonder if I have been too harsh. Maybe it's the religion she believes in that has made her the kind of girl she is."

Prompted by that thought as he arrived in Australia, he hunted up our Latter-day Saint boys. We had a chaplain over there. He began to attend and he began to ask questions and finally on her birthday he was baptized and he sent her his picture with his baptismal certificate as a birthday present and with it a letter in which he said, "I am going to try hard to live as a Latter-day Saint should so that when I get back home I will be worthy to be ordained an elder so I can take you to the House of the Lord where at last you and I can have that eternal marriage which you have planned for so long." There is the application of that principle in that lovely girl. Her eye was ever fixed single to that eternal glory, the exaltation of which could not be gained except by an eternal marriage. [*Harold B. Lee* 4]

Dangers of Marrying Out of the Church. I gave a talk, I believe it was last conference, on partnership between parents in the home, and I had a letter the other day from a young woman who had read it. I had counseled in that talk that our young folks marry within the Church. This young woman said in her letter that she had married out of the Church, but that she was fortunate in getting a very fine man and that after a few years of married life she converted him. They have been to the temple, and she is extremely happy. Now she questioned whether or not we should give counsel for our young people to marry within the Church.

Well, I haven't answered yet, and when I do I'll say to her that her case is a great exception. One time we had a survey made, and we discovered that the number of young women who married out of the Church who converted their husbands was almost infinitesimally small. The number of young men who married out of the Church converted their wives in larger percentages. But for happiness, happiness throughout life, I must still stand by the counsel we have given that young people have a common understanding with common ideals of the great principles of life, in order that they may enjoy compatibility and a common purpose toward which they may work. I still think it well to counsel our young folk to marry within the Church, and of course, you know the kind of marriage that is altogether most desirable. I trust that all have that ideal. [*Stephen L Richards* 4]

I was attending a conference in Chicago a few years ago. There was a young woman sitting on about the third row back with a baby in her arms, in a white shawl. She came up after the meeting and said, "Brother Richards, I would like to meet you."

And I said, "I would like to meet you."

Then she started to weep, and I said, "I'll bet you are a western girl, aren't you?" She couldn't talk; she just nodded. I said, "And you married out of the Church?" I got another nod. And I said, "And your husband doesn't like you to come to Church?" I got another nod. And then I said, "And you are homesick—homesick for your Church, and for your people." With that she dropped down on the front bench and hid her face in the shawl and wept like her little heart would break. You know, you can't run away from God. You can't run away from these things that are sacred and dear to you. And there are many, many unhappy girls in this world, who have married under conditions like that, and they have not found the happiness they thought they would find. [*LeGrand Richards* 2]

. . . I had a woman in my office to see me during the war. Her boy had gone to California in the service and had met a girl that he decided to marry. He wrote his mother and said, "Mother, the reason I like her so much is because she is so much like you." She feigned a love for the Church until she caught him, and then she did all she could to lead him away from the Church. When the first Christmas came around, even though he had never used tobacco or anything like that, she bought him a carton of cigarettes and some smoking tobacco and a pipe. That was his first Christmas from his wife, and he had never used it before, but you see, like Moses said, "She will lead away your heart from following after me, and so shall the anger of the Lord be kindled." This mother came to me brokenhearted because of the fact that this girl was trying to lead her boy away from serving the Lord as he had been taught. . . . [*LeGrand Richards* 2]

. . . A girl came to me in the South when I was president of the Mission. She was a school teacher and she said, "Brother

Richards, I am going to get married. What do you think about it?"

"Well," I said, "do I know him?"

She said "No."

Then I said, "Is he a member of the Church?"

And she said, "No."

I said, "Well, now I don't know. Maybe he is all right." I didn't dare tell her that she must marry in the Church down there because I didn't know who she would pick to marry unless she picked on the missionaries, and we had hands off signs hanging all over them. So I said this, "You are a sweet, clean, beautiful young woman, and unless he is a clean man you will never be happy with him. A beautiful clean woman cannot be happy with an unclean man any more than you can mix oil and water. And in your courtship with him you will know whether he is clean or not. You will know whether he is motivated by high and holy principles and desires or whether he is coarse, base, and tries to take advantage of you. If you marry him he must be willing to let you raise your children in the Church, because knowing as you do that Joseph Smith was a prophet and the Book of Mormon is true, that the Lord has restored his truth to the earth, unless you can plant these truths in the hearts of your children you will be a very unhappy woman."

Then I said, "He must be a prayerful man because as wicked as the world is today, I would not trust any man to be true to his wife unless he believes that there is a God and that someday he will have to account to God for what he does and how he lives."

I didn't see her again for several months, when I went back to hold a conference in that part of the mission. She came in during the morning session, her train was late, and after the meeting she came up and reached out her hand and I said, "Name, please."

"Oh, I am still Miss so and so."

"Well, what became of the marriage?"

She said, "President Richards, he didn't come up to your specifications."

I told that story in Alabama a few months after that, and at the close of the meeting a seventeen-year-old girl came up and said, "President Richards, if I had heard that story six months ago, I would be an unmarried woman today." You see, it did not take that seventeen-year-old Mormon girl very long to find out that she could not find happiness with an unclean man. [*LeGrand Richards* 2]

Importance of Mature Attitude Toward Marriage. Last winter, a student came to me. He said, "Our marriage is on the rocks. We've been married a year and a half; we have a baby, and now we have nothing in common." He said, "I'm a junior science student; I come home from school and work—there's no dinner there. I have to go down to the store often and buy a can of soup and open it for supper. I try to get my wife to go to Church with me and work with me, and she has no interest. We try to read books together —she won't read; she won't listen. She says she has no motivation for anything that I think is good in life. She wants me to quit school, get a job, and take things easier."

I said to him. "Tell me about your courtship. How did you court?"

He said, "We knew each other two years; one year at high school and one year at the university."

"And what did you do?"

He said, "We danced; we went to shows; we held hands; we went to football games; we kissed each other; we petted."

They were married in the temple. They are both Latter-day Saints, and he's one of the finest boys I've had the privilege to teach. (His wife I do not know.) He's a wonderful chap. I think he had a sort of blind faith, that if you're married in the temple, if you're a pretty good

Latter-day Saint in general, you'll be happily married; you'll be blessed in every particular. I don't believe that. He doesn't either any more. When you get married, you have to share life together, as some of you people know. You have to share ideas. You have to work and think together, and be good Christians. And people who court only on the basis of recreation and romance have no guarantee whatever that they will be blessed with a happy marriage. They don't fulfill the purposes of courtship, and therefore they gamble their happiness in marriage.

. . . If people could only develop Christian qualities of character first, and then become good friends before they become sweethearts, marriage would have a foundation as firm as a pyramid, and romance would sweeten and enrich the Christian life and friendship of the couple. [*Lowell L. Bennion*]

Importance of Marriage Covenant. For the proper solution of the great problem of marriage we may turn with safety to Jesus our guide. He declared that the marriage relation is of divine origin, and that marriage is ordained of God; that only under the most exceptional conditions should it be set aside. In the teachings of the Church of Christ, the family assumes supreme importance in the development of the individual and of society. "Happy and thrice happy are they who enjoy an uninterrupted union and whose love, unbroken by any complaints, shall not dissolve until the last day." And we shall add, "it shall not dissolve through all eternity."

The marriage ceremony when it is sealed by the authority of the holy priesthood endures, as do family relationships, throughout time and all eternity. "What therefore God has joined together let no man put asunder." [*David O. McKay* 3]

Purposes of Marriage. Marriage offers an opportunity to share in the love and care of children, and that is the purpose of marriage. It is for husbands and wives, yes, but it is also for the children. [*David O. McKay* 3]

Marriage and a Church Institution of Education. I would like now to draw your attention to wisdom about marriage. I understand that is not an unpopular subject on this [the BYU] campus. I am glad that it is so, and I do not mind our university acquiring the reputation of a marriage-making institution. We draw students from the stakes and missions of the Church in many parts of the world. In some sections, particularly in missions, our young folk have very little contact with those of their own age who are trained in the doctrines and practices of the Church. I think it fortunate that many may come from these isolated communities of the Church and meet with those who share their own ideals, and I resent the imputation made by some that this providential meeting of young compatible people is a deterrent to the acquisition of a good, sound education. A young man or a young woman may come here and get a good education, and if he or she gets a good mate in the process, the student who is so fortunate would be well justified in paying two or three times the tuition we charge. [*Stephen L Richards* 3]

Death and Resurrection

Two Deaths. The Fall of Adam brought two deaths into the world. Before the Fall, Adam and Eve walked and talked with God in the Garden. The Fall took them away from the presence of God. That was a spiritual death and comes to be known in our scriptures as the second death.

The other death was the mortal death. Our bodies die and go back to mother earth from which they came. Unless we had been redeemed from this mortal death we could not have been reunited with our spirits, and the great plan of the Creator would have been defeated, which plan is based upon the fact, as we all know, that we lived before we came here, that we live here, tabernacled in the flesh, and that after our death, which separates spirit and body, and our body goes to the grave, there is, under the eternal plan, a reuniting of the body and of the spirit, making the perfect soul, a reuniting which gives us the power to fulfill the destiny that is ours, of eternal progression. . . .

Jesus came and lived his life through. Then he gave it, "no man took it from him," in order that you and I and all mankind might have the ability to regain our spirits and become immortal. This redeemed us from the mortal death brought by the Fall. This salvation is granted to every soul born to this earth.

The other death, the spiritual death, we, ourselves, must overcome. It is for us, ourselves, to gain our way back into the presence of God, and we do it by knowing Christ, and knowing him, then by keeping his commandments. [*J. Reuben Clark, Jr.* 1]

Purpose of Death Death has passed upon all men to fulfill the merciful plan of the Creator. Death is a part of life, the greater life. We are in one stage of life. We have passed from the spirit condition, the spirit world, into this mortal world, and through the resurrection we will pass on to the uniting of spirit and body inseparably, and if faithful to the commandments of the Lord, to receive a fullness of joy, the exaltation in the kingdom of God. [*Joseph Fielding Smith* 1]

Life's Final Examination. I heard a story over in the Hawaiian Islands last summer about a little girl who had taken her friend to her home. While they were playing about, the elderly grandmother in the home spent much of her time reading the Bible. Every time this little neighbor girl came, the grandmother was reading the Bible, and she said finally, to the little granddaughter, "Why does your grandma spend so much time reading the Bible?"

And the little granddaughter replied, "Oh, grandma's cramming for the final examination."

Well, she wasn't so far wrong. And I think it would be well if all of us would be a little more mindful of the importance of cramming for the final examination, for as the song often sung to remind us asserts, "We may be nearer home today, nearer now than we think." [*Harold B. Lee* 2]

Unfinished Business. The story opens with a young woman on the train, alone with her thoughts, on her way to visit her dying father. For the hundredth time she opened her purse, took out the telegram that read simply, "Father critically ill. Come at once. Mother," and all through the journey the daughter prayed that the Lord would keep him alive until she could arrive and see him again; then somewhat guiltily she had to say to herself, "Well, over the years we have taken father more or less just as a matter of course. He was a necessity; he provided our food and our clothes and our shelter." But somehow now to realize that he was in imminent danger of slipping away, being taken by death, caused a longing that she could be close to him again, that she could roll back the years and see him again as she had seen him in her childhood days. Her father was in a coma, still alive when she arrived, but a few hours later he slipped quietly away. She was assigned by the family to the task of going through his personal papers and taking care of what the family called the "unfinished business."

She went carefully to her task to make sure that there was nothing that he wished to have done that would be left undone. As she searched in an inside pocket of his coat, she came upon a crumpled bit of paper which showed the effects of having been removed and read, and folded and unfolded many times. This crumpled piece of paper was a message from a young girl whom her father had befriended, and this letter was a letter of appreciation to this great noble father. Although this other little girl was not his daughter, he had seemingly clung to the message which this letter conveyed as something of a satisfaction that he hadn't received from his own. The little girl had poured out her heart in gratitude that he had come at a crisis in her life, and she openly expressed her love for his thoughtfulness and kindness to her. The daughter laid down the paper and wept because she realized that his own daughter had failed to give her father what this other girl had given, and the thing for which he had longed so much. "Unfinished business," but unfortunately the kind of business that she was not permitted to finish. How she wished that she could have rolled back the clock and had a chance to live over some of the years, to have made the life of her father more happy and more joyous than she had done. [*Harold B. Lee* 2]

Education

A Desire to Become Educated. In the first place, his mother taught him [President J. Reuben Clark, Jr.] to read and write so that when he entered the grade schools he was sufficiently far advanced that he was immediately admitted to the third grade. When he finished the grade school in Tooele County there were no high schools. In order, therefore, to get all that he could out of the schooling they had, he retook the work of the eighth grade for three successive years. . . . Not until he reached the age of twenty-two did he have the opportunity to enter upon a high school course, (except for an interrupted term of four months at nineteen), but he made up quickly for lost time, because in the succeeding four years he made up his high school work, and finished his college course. In 1898 he received the degree of bachelor of science from the University of Utah with an ambition to become a specialist in mining law.

During the time he was at the University of Utah, obtaining both his high school and college work, he was employed on a job for ten hours a day at the wage of $50.00 a month. And they deducted from that $50.00 per month, all the time that he took out for his classes. So he didn't have much left. And despite the fact that he had this ten hour a day job and was pursuing both high school and college work at the same time, he was editor of the student paper, president of the studentbody, and valedictorian of his class. [*Statement about President Clark by President Ernest L. Wilkinson*]

No Easy Road to Learning. In your classes, or in your school, you probably have—we used to in my time, and I guess it has not changed too much since—you have the "snaps" in the courses and then you have some where you work. The great value of a "snap" course, I was about to say the only value, is that it gives you credit toward graduation. Loose thinking, or no thinking, is the usual thing in the "snap" courses. They are often not worth your time. Try to get your teachers to build up a little bit on it and give you something that really makes you work.

Somewhere in the school there are those who are working. They may not be your social lights, they may not always be your most brilliant associates, but they are working, and do not be surprised if, as the years roll on, they move out in front and you, who spend your time taking this other kind of course, find yourselves becoming the intellectual sewer-diggers and hod-carriers. Do not run that risk. Make your "snap" courses unpopular and they will change.

. . . I recall an old story . . . about Euclid and Pharaoh of Egypt. Pharaoh decided that he wanted to learn geometry. Now just why anybody would want to learn geometry, I do not personally know, but some like it. Pharaoh evidently thought he liked it and so he asked Euclid to teach it to him. He took two or three lessons and then called in Euclid and said to him something like this: "Now, look here, boy, this is altogether too hard work for a Pharaoh. I want an easy way so that I can pick up this geometry in just a few lessons."

And Euclid is said to have replied to him, "Your majesty, there is no royal road to geometry." There is no royal road to any learning, no matter what it is. There is no royal road to any righteous living, no matter who you are or where you are. There is no royal road to anything that is worth while. Nothing that is deserving of earning or of cherishing comes except through hard work. I care not how much of a genius you may be, the rule will still hold. [*J. Reuben Clark, Jr.* 3]

Education Requires Effort. Humble, prayerful considera-ation compels us to conclude that the knowledge necessary for our eternal salvation cannot be had without effort com-mensurate with the result desired. [*Henry D. Moyle* 4]

Purpose of Education. George E. Stoddard, well-known educator, says that the aim of education is to develop a structure of thought and to improve human relations. A university is not a dictionary, a dispensary, nor is it a de-partment store. It is more than a storehouse of knowledge, and more than a community of scholars. University life is essentially an exercise in thinking, preparing and living. Without further comment, I give you this definition: The aim of education is to develop resources in the child that will contribute to his well-being as long as life endures; to develop virile manhood, beautiful womanhood, that in every child and every youth may be found at least the promise of a friend, a companion, one who later may be fit for husband or wife, an exemplary father, or a loving intelligent mother, one who can face life with courage, meet disaster with forti-tude, and face death without fear. [*David O. McKay* 1]

. . . the highest aim in education is the awakening in the minds of youth a desire to live nobly. [*David O. McKay* 2]

The Scientific Method. It seems proper to me that Latter-day Saints approach their many problems, not only through study of the scriptures, accompanied by faith and prayer for divine inspiration, but through research in library, lab-oratory, and the out-of-doors, carefully checking and re-checking the data, integrating, interpreting, formulating theories in all the light that can be shed upon the subject, employing these theories as temporary scaffolding, to be removed and rebuilt in the light of new knowledge and ex-panded understanding. This has been the method of science, which has born much good fruit. [*Henry J. Nicholes*]

Scope of Education. Of course we all want to extend the aims of higher education beyond the cultivation of the intellect to the discovery and fulfillment of man's ultimate purpose in the universe and the preparation for life in a free society. [*Henry D. Moyle* 5]

Knowledge Is Power. Never forget that knowledge is power in the Church just as it is in the academic or the secular world. That man who has the knowledge the Lord has made available to him, who understands and explains in charity, has a remarkable advantage over the one who is ignorant. [*Stephen L Richards* 3]

Education an Obligation. Some still think of education as a luxury and a privilege, when in fact it is an obligation and a necessity. It has been said college is not an end in itself, but the means to an end, the preparation for life, not the final experience. [*Henry D. Moyle* 5]

Responsibilities of a Religious Teacher. To live an upright life, to conform to high ethical standards is the responsibility and duty of every teacher in the land. Greater even than this is the responsibility of the religious teacher. His profession is higher than that of the teacher in the common school, for in addition to his belief in the efficacy of ethical and moral precepts, a religious teacher assumes the responsibility of leading the youth into the realms of spirituality. His duty, comporting with his pretensions and profession, is to open the eyes of the blind that they may see God. What is there in man so worthy of honor and reverence as this, that he is capable of contemplating something higher than his own reason, more sublime than the whole universe, that Spirit which alone is self-subsistant, from which all truth proceeds, without which there is no truth. Leading youth to know God, to have faith in his laws, to have confidence in his fatherhood and to find solace and peace in his love— this is the greatest privilege, the most sublime opportunity offered the true educator. [*David O. McKay* 1]

Mediocre teachers are satisfied with the teaching of a few facts. That kind of teaching splinters the continuity of education, loses the value of generalization and falls short of achieving the purpose of education, namely, to transform and improve the lives of young people.

Great teachers teach facts and experiences just as do mediocre teachers, but they do not stop there. They organize and spiritualize these facts in such a way as to produce understanding of principles. Understanding of principles leads to proper attitudes and proper attitudes result in improved behavior. [*Henry Aldous Dixon*]

Tribute to a Great Teacher. I went one day to the Island of Maui. I was going to speak to the students of the oldest college in those islands. The young man who was the valedictorian at the graduating exercise made an exceptionally fine address. After the exercises were over, I followed him up the walk. I congratulated him. "I would like to ask you a personal question. Do you mind?"

"No," he said, "go ahead."

"Could you tell me who your grandparents were?"

"Yes. A Norwegian sailor, a Portugese woman, on my grandfather's side, and on my grandmother's side a Chinese man, a Hawaiian woman—these were my grandparents."

"Well," I said, "with all this blood surging in your veins—who are you?"

I remember he straightened up, he stopped in his walking and looked at me with pride and said, "I'm a pure American."

I went down to the office of the principal of the school and said to him, "I've been deeply impressed with a young man that I have met here at your school."

"You mean the young man who gave the valedictory address?"

"Yes," I said.

"Well, if you can just keep him balanced, he's going to be a great fellow some day. Just recently he received a check for $750; he won the American Legion prize essay, entitled 'Why I am an American.' "

Well, I looked for him again, and after a little while I saw him on the campus. "It's about thirty or forty minutes before the plane goes—are you busy?"

"No," he said, "I've been looking for you. I want you to go with me. It will be quite a hike. I want to go up on the side of the mountain." As we went along he said, "I'm going to introduce you to someone. This will not be a personal introduction, but I hope it will be interesting. I want to tell you something about this individual. He came to this school when he was twenty-eight years old. It was a new experience for him to go to school. But he had two things that he has implanted in our hearts. They were a love for the Hawaiian people and love for their crafts—the things they make with their hands. We treasure his memory here at this school. It was sometime ago when he was with us, but to every student here at Maui, his story is told; he still stays with us."

Looking back to see the vista and at a point in the bend of the trail, we stopped and suddenly we faced a granite slab. Now he stood back and let me go forward alone and on this granite slab were these words. "David Maulo—In Us You Live Again." What a magnificent tribute to any member of a faculty, or the president of a university to whom it can be truly said, by his students, "In Us You Live Again."

Here is where your dreams come true. Here is where the things for which you have prayed and worked shall live again. I was so deeply impressed by it. Soon we walked down the trail again, and off I went flying to another island. [*Oscar A. Kirkham*]

Liberal Education. The sure weapon against bad ideas is better ideas. The source of better ideas is wisdom, and the surest path to wisdom is a liberal education. [*Henry D. Moyle* 5]

Men are men before they are lawyers, physicians, engineers, manufacturers. They should all have a liberal education for a foundation. If you make them capable and sensible men, they will make themselves competent professional men. [*Henry D. Moyle* 5]

Education for "Life." I have a friend who is a farmer. He thinks that he has to work from sundown to sunup (or the other way around) without ever giving anything else a thought. In the morning he gets up and he sits down to the breakfast table. . . . His wife has already been up half an hour slaving over a hot stove in the kitchen, so that she can provide him with his ham and eggs and a stack of wheats, or something of the sort, . . . He sits there, eats his breakfast, reaches for the morning paper, glances over that.

Then he starts out into the field somewhere, busies himself all day long, takes along a cold lunch that he eats around twelve or one o'clock, comes home at night around six or seven; he and the rest of the people on the farm do the chores, so-called, and he comes in and sits down in a chair. His wife, in the meantime, has prepared a good heavy supper for him. He takes down the supper, reaches for the evening paper and glances over that a little—sees what the headlines are, anyway. By that time he sits in his over-stuffed chair in his front room and tries to finish the paper. At about 8:30 p.m. his wife nudges him, and says, "John, if you're going to sit here and sleep, you might just as well go to bed."

So John goes to bed about nine o'clock. He wakes up about four-thirty or five in the morning and, still half asleep, goes through the same rigmarole again that day. About Sunday, when time comes that he should go to church, he can't go to church, because the weather looks threatening and he has to get his hay in, right then.

That's the way it goes from day to day, week to week. Now I ask you: Do you call that living? He makes good money; he pays a large income tax, but I am sure that you or I would not want to exchange our lots for his. I am sure that that man is not "living" in any sense of the word. He's simply providing food and clothing and shelter for himself and his family, but there is not much in his life that he needed to come to this earth for, as far as I'm concerned.

You can see from this extreme counterpart of what I call "life," that perhaps if you or I were asked, "What are the necessities of life?" we would go far beyond specifying simply food, shelter, and clothing. There are certain things that people generally call cultural that have long ago become necessities to you and to me.

I hope that you will, whenever you're tempted to turn down an opportunity to expand your knowledge of the best that has been thought and done in this world, remember that perhaps, after all, those things are more important to you in your life ultimately than this immediate provision of food, clothing, and shelter. [*Gerrit de Jong, Jr.*]

Results of Religious Training. It became my duty to go up from London to a large military camp near Liverpool on one occasion. I sent word ahead Saturday night that I would be there Sunday morning. I sent the word to the chaplain who was in charge of the area. When I arrived, just outside of the hut where we were going to hold the meeting there were seventy-five LDS servicemen. Quite a number of them were in battledress, which indicated they were just leaving for or returning from the continent on bombing missions. The chaplain said to me, "I'm very happy to tell you, Mr. Brown, that there are seventy-five men here and there are only seventy-six Mormons in this camp. The other boy is in the hospital." He said, "You gave less than twenty-four hours notice, and you have seventy-five out of seventy-six present."

When we went into this meeting I didn't know any of the boys by name, but I said, "How many are there here who have been on missions?" A number of hands went up. I said, "How many of you have been through seminary or institutes of religion at home?" Again many hands were raised. Then I asked for the number of elders present. I think with those three questions I had the show of hands of everybody there. And then taking a chance I said, "Will *you*, and *you*, and *you*, and *you* come up and administer to the sacrament? And will *you* come and lead the music? And who can play one of these portable organs?" Several hands were raised and the boys came up.

One of the men who was administering to the sacrament was dressed in battledress. As he knelt, he said, "O God the Eternal Father"—and then his voice broke. He paused, I think, for a full minute, and then he went on and blessed the bread. Breaking the thread of my story for a minute I'd like to tell you this: I went to that boy after the meeting and I said, "What is the matter, lad? What choked you up?"

"Well, sir," he said, "a few hours ago I was flying back from Germany in a bomber. My tail assembly was pretty well shot away. One of my engines was out. It didn't look like it was possible for me to get across that channel. Remembering things I learned in seminary, Sunday School, at home and in the Church, I looked up and I said, 'O God, please come to my rescue.'" He added, "Sir, I haven't mentioned God's name since then until I mentioned it here on my knees, and I just had to stop long enough to say, 'thank you, God.'"

Well, we went on with our meeting. I said, "Will *you* come and speak and *you* and *you*." These boys came up. And I want to tell you young people that I've attended meetings in the Salt Lake Tabernacle, and in the Salt Lake Temple and other temples and other places throughout the Church, and I've heard the best speakers we have, but if you would like to hear the gospel preached from way down deep in the souls of men, you call on a group like that without any notice and ask them to bear their testimonies and tell what they believe. There was a spirit in that meeting which moved my friend the chaplain so deeply he turned to me after the meeting and said, "This is the greatest experience of my life." [*Hugh B. Brown* 1]

The Role of the Brigham Young University in Church Education.   The position of the Brigham Young University among the universities of the world is certainly a distinctive one. We have only one justification for our existence here as a college of higher learning. That is because the Church of which this great institution is a part has the truth. We seek in this school to teach the truth as it can be taught nowhere else in the world. There is no other university willing to accept the revealed word of God as it has been given to mankind in these latter days as we do here. And we should permit all of our work to be tempered with the thought that there is no truth to which we can not attain through our own diligence if we but have the faith and the courage and the determination and the persistence to follow through and to obtain it. [*Henry D. Moyle* 3]

The underlying educational concept at Brigham Young University is twofold: first, the orderly development of the mind, the intelligence with which God has endowed his children; and secondly, the acquisition of knowledge and skills devoted to the blessing of humanity and the building of our Father's Kingdom in the earth. [*Stephen L Richards* 2]

What is the overall objective, the central aim of the educational processes carried forward at the Brigham Young University and in the Church School System?

A commonly given and correct answer is: to make Latter-day Saints. I would like to break down that answer into at least a few of its component parts. First, I bring forward as a central aim, to help younger people, and older ones as well, to acquire wisdom. The ancient scriptures, supported by modern revelations, have characterized wisdom as the principal thing to be acquired in a lifetime. Sometimes the word *wisdom* seems to have a formidable aspect for youth.

Now, so that wisdom may not seem formidable to young folk, I propose a simpler, and I think more understandable, definition and concept of it. I think we may well look upon wisdom as the capacity to make intelligent and beneficial decisions. . . . Wisdom is the beneficent application of principle to decision, and of course, that concept of wisdom postulates the necessity of acquiring and knowing principles, and . . . we cannot know principles and understand their derivation and impact on life without acquiring knowledge, which comes to us in good measure out of study in the educational process. [*Stephen L Richards* 3]

You remember that the Lord said that the glory of God is intelligence and that we cannot be saved in ignorance. That gives education a position of prime importance among the Latter-day Saints. The brethren have established this great University [BYU] and the other sections of our educational system, with one great purpose being to provide education in an atmosphere which will foster faith in God and which will avoid subjecting the students to worldly influences which might destroy their faith and their morals. Another great purpose in the establishment of this school was to provide the type of education which will give students the proper perspective on life, helping them to evaluate accurately the experiences which come to them and thus serve to guide them properly. To accomplish these great purposes we have established this school which is high in scholarship, high in standards, noble in tradition. [*Mark E. Petersen* 4]

It is a joy to know that here at Brigham Young University increased attention is being given to one of what I consider the three great objectives of this institution. The

first objective, I think, is to help build real Latter-day Saints
—men and women who live according to the standards of
the Church and Kingdom of God. Second, to train young
men and women for honorable vocations and for life. And
third, to teach the responsibilities of citizenship. This includes an understanding of the principles of Americanism,
and a love for the Constitution of this land and the glorious
concepts and principles embodied in that great document.
It also means to teach something of the prophetic history
of this great nation and of the fruits of our free enterprise
system. All of these may be encompassed in this one
thought: *teaching the responsibilities of citizenship.* [*Ezra
Taft Benson* 2]

The unique commission of . . . the Brigham Young
University, has always been and now is threefold. First,
to help you recognize that there are two sources of learning,
one divine, the other human; second, to urge and inspire
you students to drink deeply from both sources; and third,
to teach and train you to correctly distinguish between the
learning of the world and revealed truth, that you may not
be deceived in your search. [*Marion G. Romney* 6]

Influence of Brigham Young University. You know, I have
always had a deep reverence for the Brigham Young University. With thousands of others, I believe it is the Lord's
University. I have a wholesome respect and appreciation for
all institutions of learning, but the BYU is unique in all
the world, having been founded by a Prophet of the Lord—
and from that time until the present it has been directed
by Prophets of the Living God, with members of the
Quorum of the Twelve as its Board of Directors. I am grateful for the influence of the BYU in the lives of our children
and their companions. Its inspired instructors here have
shared with our home and our Church, the responsibility
of giving direction and purpose to their lives. Each and every
subject taught has been additionally enlightened by the

spirit of truth which permeates this divinely established institution. [*Lavina Fugal*]

Attitude toward Secular Learning. Another problem I should like to pose is this: Just how strongly do we at BYU believe in secular learing? We have the contradiction here of often discrediting the learning of men, implying that it is sometimes evil and dangerous, and yet giving education in a broad sense an important place in the gospel plan. It's rather paradoxical: We build a beautiful science building to house men of competence in these branches of learning, and then discredit the type of learning that we would glorify in that temple of learning. Frankly, the purpose of this university is to find an integration of truth, and that means we should respect truth from all sources. There is no monopoly in this wonderful field of truth seeking.

But, the student is often torn between efforts to discredit one kind of learning or another. What does this conflict do to your achievements? Do we seek short-cuts to the learning process? A student complained to me when I was putting him through some pretty difficult requirements in a course, that he couldn't see anything to this stuff about the laws of learning I was trying to teach him. He said, "All learning is of the spirit of the Lord. And we don't need to follow these laws of learning." I hope this is not a very common misunderstanding, because I am as sure as that I stand here, that the Lord does not intend people to circumvent the laws of learning in either religious or secular fields. We pay a price for our development, and that price is work! That is the genius of our religious philosophy—that we grow, and we grow through the making of good choices and through individual effort. [*Mark K. Allen*]

Another problem, which I hope will be understandable to you when I speak of it, and which I fear might be termed almost world-wide, is something of a movement of anti-intellectualism. People, for various reasons, perhaps with the very best of motives, question what is being done by educators and question the wisdom of educational processes. Such questions are often justified, but not to the extent that they impede the progress of education. There are also people who, when you talk to them in the abstract, will say, "Surely, we believe in education; we believe we should have good opportunities for students and good opportunities for teachers." However, when these same people are asked to be more specific, they are often quite ready to refute their earlier generalizations. [*George Albert Smith, Jr.*]

Attitude toward Authority. We are members of a church in which there is properly great respect for authority. In your scholastic lives you will frequently be put in positions where you do and should challenge authority. Here again you should develop your own self-confidence and feel that your ideas are as good as anyone's at the appropriate times. When the basic fundamentals of the Church are involved, although it may be difficult for us to do so, we submit to the teachings and views of our authorities. But in matters which are in the general realms of science and learning, we are not being disrespectful if we challenge the views of other people and see if we can improve upon them.

This brings us to the twin problems of having strong convictions versus being open-minded. Certainly, on the fundamental matters of life and those which involve our faith and conduct, we should all have strong convictions. However, on many other matters in life we are ill-advised to close our minds; we should keep them open so that we may learn.

* * *

So, you are faced with these conflicts: authority versus self-confidence, open-mindedness versus conviction. And you will frequently find yourself in positions in which you should be not at all ashamed to say, "This is what the Church teaches, and I accept it. This is what some other facts seem to prove, and I do not denounce those who have concluded it. I am aware of what they say; I am cognizant of it." There appears here to be a dilemma. Do not be embarrassed to take this viewpoint. You will have it from time to time, so accept it as one of the experiences of life. As all of us become wiser, some of these dilemmas, some of these seeming conflicts, will disappear to a substantial degree. [*George Albert Smith, Jr.*]

Eternal Life

Eternal Life Based on Personal Progress. Eternal life, the greatest of all the gifts of God, is the need of all the children of God. It is available to every man and woman by obedience to the laws and ordinances of the gospel. And this means, to quote the Lord: "Ye must serve me with all your heart, might, mind and strength." And to me this is the description of spiritual work. The good way of life will always provide the maximum incentive for individual growth and development. The good individual will constantly strive to expand his talents. And then will our minds and our spirits, and our ability to love and to serve "blossom as a rose," and we will be blessed according to our needs. It is a basic principle of the gospel. It is a principle that all must accept, and only those who accept will be among those who harvest the choice blessings which the Lord has to give. [*William F. Edwards*]

Trials and Eternal Life. Should we be protected always from hardship, pain, suffering, sacrifice or labor? Should the Lord protect the righteous? Should he immediately punish the wicked? If growth comes from fun and ease and aimless irresponsibility, then why should we ever exert ourselves to work or learn or overcome? If success is measured by the years we live, then early death is failure and tragedy. If earth life is the ultimate, how can we justify death ever, even in old age? If we look at mortality as a complete existence, then pain, sorrow, failure, and short life could be a calamity. But if we look upon the whole life as an eternal thing stretching far into the pre-mortal past and into the eternal post-death future, then all happenings may be in proper perspective and may fall into proper place.

Is there not wisdom in His giving us trials that we might rise above them, responsibilities that we might achieve, work that we might harden our muscles, sorrows that we might have our souls tried? Were we not permitted temptations to test our strength, sickness that we might learn patience, death that we might be immortalized and glorified? [*Spencer W. Kimball 2*]

Two Classes in the Hereafter. It should be remembered that those who enter the next life are divided into two classes, (1) those who obtain immortality, which is the power to live forever, but banished from the presence of the Eternal Father, and (2) those who obtain eternal life, which will take them back into the presence of the Father and the Son to dwell in immortal glory. [*Joseph Fielding Smith 2*]

Faith

A Simple Faith.   I assure you that however much you study and reflect, if you hold to the truths that Jesus taught, you will take them on faith and not on rationalizing. So I urge you not to be too much concerned if you cannot understand by your reason the things which Jesus taught, the principles and the doctrines of the Restored Gospel. I urge you not to be too concerned if you find it impossible, perhaps, to rationalize the First Vision, to rationalize the restoration of the Aaronic and the Melchizedek Priesthoods. Take them as facts and build thereon, because if you undertake to rationalize you are too likely to lose your faith. . . . Cease your rationalizing. Take this simple faith. It will give you hope, it will give you courage, it will give you determination; it will give you more joy than you ever can get in any other way. [*J. Reuben Clark, Jr.* 2]

Importance of Faith.   Faith is the foundation of all righteousness. It justly claims first place in any plan designed to unfold to the understanding of man, the nature, the personality, the purposes of God. The prime cause of faith in Christ must arise out of a desire to be happy in this life and to become more intelligent, and to progress toward a higher life. [*Henry D. Moyle* 4]

Purpose of Faith.   To bring to pass our complete salvation and give us needed experience that could not be obtained in the world of spirits, preparation was made for us to come to this earth where we obtain bodies of flesh and bones and pass through a short period of mortality where we are tried and proven to see if we will be true to all divine commandments in this mortal state, walking by faith, and not by sight. In the spirit existence, we walked by sight in the divine presence of our Eternal Father. In mortal life which was prepared for us, we are walking by faith through the guidance of divine revelation coming through chosen prophets who receive commandments from the Lord. [*Joseph Fielding Smith* 2]

Mature Faith. . . . I'm sure that people who are loyal to religion in general, who participate in the Church, who have faith in the gospel, are likely to find peace of mind and a drive which will help them to be successful in all areas of life of which we have spoken. But let us not use our faith as a blind substitute for knowledge. Let us not use our faith as a substitute for obedience to the principles of life. Rather, let us let our faith inspire us to seek eagerly to understand life, and to live in harmony with our understanding of its principles and values.

* * *

I don't believe that peace is going to come, between labor and capital for instance, or among the nations of the earth, because we Latter-day Saints live a good personal, religious life, because we pray for peace, because we keep the Word of Wisdom, or because we work in and are loyal to the Church. I think those things are wonderful, but we must go beyond that, I think that we have to learn which principles of the gospel can be applied to economic relations to bring peace among men. [*Lowell L. Bennion*]

Faith versus Sight. In our ante-mortal state we walked by sight. Then we knew God. We lived with him. He was our father, and our teacher. This earth life was intended as a place where we might learn to walk just a little way by faith. . . . [*Sterling W. Sill* 2]

Two Purposes of Mortal Life. We came to this world for two great purposes: one, to get these tabernacles of flesh and bones; the other, to pass through a period of probation, of testing, to see whether or not we will be willing to keep the commandments of God, walking by faith and not by sight. [*Joseph Fielding Smith* 3]

Naive versus Mature Faith. A few years ago in Idaho, a young couple were married in the Idaho Falls Temple. After a strenuous wedding day, they set out for their honeymoon. They decided to drive some distance that night. They crashed into a bridge and the boy was killed. The family was grieved, of course, for none could understand why this young man, who had fulfilled a mission and was a fine Latter-day Saint, should be killed on his wedding night. His mother wrung her hands, and the bride was trying to blame herself, wondering just why it had happened. I don't know why it happened. God may have had a hand in it. I'm sure it wasn't to punish the mother or the boy. I think the easiest explanation might be that this boy drove when he was sleepy and tired, violating the rules of safe driving, and had to pay the price. At least, that's the explanation that you and I can profit from most and do something about in our own living.

My thought is this, students, that I think sometimes we Latter-day Saints have a sort of naive faith, a blind faith. We feel that if we live our religion in general, if we are pretty good Latter-day Saints in some particulars, we shall be blessed in all things. And I doubt that very much. I'm reminded of the verse in the Doctrine and Covenants which goes something like this, "There is a law irrevocably decreed before the foundations of the earth upon which every blessing is predicated. And when we receive any blessing from God it is by obedience to *that* law, (that particular law) upon which it is predicated." If we want a safe trip we'd better not only pray, but drive carefully and follow the rules of the road. [*Lowell L. Bennion*]

Faith and Works. Now there must be a certain necessary preparation before you can receive divine communications. The Lord expects you and me to seek and to knock and to do and to keep his commandments if we would know, and to do all we can that lies within our power before we seek spiritual help. I remember, to illustrate what I mean, a sister coming to my office some years ago. She was an elderly sister and was troubled with a serious heart ailment. Her children had urged her to go to a doctor and the doctor had prescribed some kind of heart stimulant, I suppose digitalis, or something akin to it. But she had resisted the idea. She said, "I have the faith that if I can receive a blessing I won't need any medicine." And so she had come to me to stand out against the doctor and her family and make it unnecessary for her to be so treated. I said I would like to read her something that Brigham Young said. He came to a home of some people who were ill, they were troubled with some kind of intestinal disorder. He said to the mother:

Have you used any remedies?

We wish the elders to lay hands upon us, and we have faith that we shall be healed.

That is very inconsistent according to my faith. If we are sick, and ask the Lord to heal us, and to do all for us that is necessary to be done, according to my understanding of the Gospel of salvation, I might as well ask the Lord to cause my wheat and corn to grow, without my plowing the ground and casting in the seed. It appears consistent to me to apply every remedy that comes within the range of my knowledge, and to ask my Father in Heaven, in the name of Jesus Christ, to sanctify that application to the healing of my body; to another this may appear inconsistent.

But supposing we were traveling in the mountains, and all we had or could get, in the shape of nourishment, was a little venison, and one or two were taken sick, without anything in the world in the shape of healing medicine within our reach, what should we do? According to my faith, ask the Lord Almighty to send an angel to heal the sick. This is our privilege, when so situated that we cannot get anything to help ourselves. Then the Lord and his servants can do all. But it is my duty to do, when I have it in my power. 4:24 (*Discourses of Brigham Young*, pages 251-252)

[*Harold B. Lee* 5]

Live for Your Faith. A great deal also has been said about giving your life for the work, not in death, but in living day by day. It is so easy sometimes to die; it is hard sometimes to live the principles for which we stand. What we need today is character. What we need is devotion, loyalty, a willingness to stand by our guns and fight and live and then, if called upon, to die—to hold fast the faith. . . . I believe it is far more important to live for our faith than to die for our faith. . . . [*Mark E. Petersen* 6]

Faith, a Fundamental Principle. . . . every developed religion is characterized by three essential doctrines—its doctrine of *God;* its doctrine of *Sin and Salvation;* its doctrine of *Immortality.* No religion is worth the name that does not emphasize those three fundamentals. Out of that, under the doctrine of sin and salvation, come many principles applicable to daily life. It is these principles, and the application of these principles, which determine the happiness, the success or the misery and failure of the individual. . . . And great men, fellow students, prove the efficacy, the applicability of these ideals of the gospel. Take, for example, *faith.* In our Church we emphasize the principle of faith in God, as do other churches. It comes to that fundamental principle. We may discuss what it is; people may doubt its power as an active principle; but the great men of the world recognize its effect upon the spiritual growth of man. You recall the words of Dryden ["Religio Laici"]:

Dim as the borrowed rays of moon and stars to
lonely, weary, wandering travelers,
Is reason to the soul; and as on high those rolling
fires discover but the sky,
Not light us here, so Reason's glimmering ray was
lent not to assure our doubtful way,
But lead us upward to a brighter day.

And as those nightly tapers disappear,
When day's bright lord ascends our hemisphere,
So pale grows Reason at Religion's sight,
So dies and so dissolves in supernatural light.
In this wild maze their vain endeavors end:
How can the less the greater comprehend?
Or finite Reason reach Infinity?
For what could fathom God were more than He.

[*David O. McKay*]

Free Agency

Growth through Free Agency. Before the creation began, of the world—you have heard of the Great Council of Heaven then held. . . . You recall that there were two great principles upon which two great Sons of God took opposite views: one was the question of the glory of God, which meant his power; and the other was free agency. Satan, as you know, wanted God to give up his power; and let him, Satan, take his place. I do not wish to speak irreverently, but I can think of Satan as feeling that perhaps God was a little old-fashioned, a little too old; the time needed some new blood, some new ideas; and so he advanced the new idea that men should be deprived of their agency, their free agency, which they possessed, and by reason of which, only, Satan was able to advance the thoughts which he expressed.

The other Son was our Lord and Master who came to earth and became known as Jesus, and was entitled, also, the *Christ*. He said to the Father, . . . "I will go; I will act as your agent; I will use your power, but it will be your power. I will give to men their free agency. They may serve or disserve, as they may determine." And, incidentally, there is no growth on this earth, intellectually or otherwise, save by the exercise of our free agency, by our choosing our own course and growing in it. [*J. Reuben Clark, Jr.* 2]

Accepting God's Commandments. We have the divinely given right and also the individual responsibility of deciding whether we will accept or whether we will reject the laws and commandments of God. Acceptance brings freedom, peace of mind, and joy in the extreme. [*ElRay L. Christiansen* 2]

Free Agency a Great Gift. We have no right—we have the privilege but no right—to do wrong. No man has the right to violate a commandment that God has given us, but he has his agency. He may be true and faithful in the keeping of the commandments of the Lord, or he may reject them. The free agency which we have is one of the greatest gifts of God, the power to make our own choice. [*Joseph Fielding Smith* 3]

Life a Period of Trial. Earth life is a period of trial for every person, not by fire or water but by two mighty forces pulling in opposite directions. On the one hand is the power of Christ and his righteousness. On the other hand are Satan and his fellow travelers. Men, in the exercise of their God-given moral agency, must determine to travel in company with the one or the other. The reward for following the one is the fruit of the Spirit—peace. The reward for following the other is the works of the flesh—the antithesis of peace. [*Marion G. Romney* 3]

Freedom in Bondage. Just as following wrong alternatives restricts free agency and leads to slavery, so pursuing correct alternatives widens the scope of one's agency and leads to perfect liberty. As a matter of fact, one may, by this process, obtain freedom of the soul while at the same time being denied political, economic and personal liberty. [*Marion G. Romney* 2]

Obeying God's Laws. As we attain that position in life where we are permitted to choose, to decide for ourselves, it is essential that we understand the difference between right and wrong, good and evil. We come to know that we are children of God, that he knows us—knows why we are here, and expects something of us. We find that he too has established laws, rules, regulations governing life, and these we try to observe because we love and honor him and have confidence that his laws were instituted for our good and happiness. [*Hugh B. Brown* 2]

The Ten Commandments. The Ten Commandments are not rules to obey as a personal favor to God. They are the fundamental principles without which mankind cannot live together. They make of those who keep them faithfully, strong, wholesome, confident, dedicated men and women. This is so because the Commandments come from the same Divine Hand that fashioned our human nature.

We cannot break the Ten Commandments. We can only break ourselves against them—or else, by keeping them, rise through them to the fullness of freedom under God. God means us to be free. With divine daring, he gave us the power of choice. [*Cecil B. DeMille*]

Progress Based upon Right Choices. We know through the revelations of God that he is the literal Father of the spirits of all men, and that all men are therefore brothers. We know that our Heavenly Father created this earth for a dwelling place for his children; that the basic purpose of our life here is to learn to keep his commandments; that we are here in mortality to be tested, and the testing requires that there be alternatives to choose among. We know that men are free agents and may (and must) choose what they will be and become and represent. We are assured that all of us will die as to the mortal body, and all shall be resurrected, through the atonement of Christ; that the body and spirit will be reunited as the eternal soul; that all will be judged at the bar of God; that the righteous will be righteous still and shall inherit the kingdom of God, and their joy will be full forever, for they shall have eternal opportunity for service and learning and growth, for loving companionship, for association with their Heavenly Father in his great creative activities. [*Marion D. Hanks* 3]

Segregate the Good. While it is a great blessing, it also is a tremendous responsibility to have a life to live and to direct and then to reap the fruits of life when it's over. Each of us must constantly and continually segregate the good from the bad; the right from the wrong; the desirable from the undesirable. Unless this segregation begins early in life and is continued in seriousness throughout one's life, one might head for difficulties, disappointments, and even disaster. [*ElRay L. Christiansen* 1]

Personal Responsibility for Sin. Let him who has evil tendencies be honest and acknowledge his weakness. I tell you the Lord places no sin in our lives. He has made no man wicked. We are sons and daughters of God, possessing seeds of godhood. We are not limited by instinct as are the beasts. We have godly power to grow and overcome and become perfect. Sin was permitted in the world and Satan permitted to tempt us, but we have our free agency. We may sin or live righteously, but we cannot escape responsibility. To blame our sin upon the Lord, saying it is inherent and cannot be controlled, is cheap and cowardly. To blame our sins upon our parents and our upbringing is the way of the escapist. One's parents may have failed; his backgrounds may have been frustrating, but as sons and daughters of a living God we have within ourselves the power to rise above our circumstances, to change our lives. Man *can* change human nature. Man *must* transform his life. We will be punished for our sins. We *must* accept responsibility for our sins. We *can* overcome. We *must* control and master self. [*Spencer W. Kimball* 1]

The gospel of Jesus Christ, and all that pertains to it, carries with it real responsibility. The very basis, the very existence, the very terms on which we agreed to come here, those terms which pertain to our own free agency, mean real responsibility. There was another pattern and plan proposed which could have relieved us of responsibility, in which we would have had no independent power of decision, no real responsibility for our own actions, and thereby no development and no growth and no real opportunity. But this gospel, which you and I have been blessed with a knowledge of, and which has been restored in this dispensation in its fullness and authority, is one that imposes upon every person the responsibility of knowing what he believes, and the responsibility for making the decisions of life in accordance with what he knows. [*Richard L. Evans* 3]

Freedom

Freedom and Responsibility. Well, how about freedom? Is freedom the right to do what we please? With freedom there is its concomitant, responsibility. With freedom there comes the obligation to consider that there are others in the world in whose lives our lives mean something and to whom our problems, our concerns, our joys, our sorrows, are as real as they are to us. What is freedom? Freedom is not—I can tell you this—is not the right to do what we please irrespective of what others think or feel or suffer. How do you get freedom? It's interesting to hear your people say. I ask them occasionally. Some think you get freedom with wealth, or health, or power, or education. Do these things bring freedom? In a sense, each of them contributes materially to freedom. Education frees us from ignorance, if we're really educated in truth. Health frees us from the burden of sickness and disease. But do these things really make one free? Does power or wealth? While each may contribute, they are not freedom. . . . If I know anything in this world, it is this: that freedom is what Jesus said it was—the opposite of slavery to sin. In the great sermon in the eighth chapter of John where we read: "Ye shall know the truth and the truth shall make you free," the Savior says that men who are servants to sin are the opposite of free. I'm talking about national and personal freedom, and I suggest that the basis on which they rest is the same: Righteousness and integrity and a high level of community and personal conduct. [*Marion D. Hanks* 1]

Threats to Freedom. We in America have been seeing freedom slipping away from us for several reasons:

We have made education a conforming process—conformity defined in what was and is yet a narrow pattern for a select few.

We are losing our freedom because great masses are looking upon success and happiness in terms of ease and material well-being, more luxury and entertainment, and because fewer and fewer young people feel the urge and are enthusiastic about the delivery of a masterful product, where achievement reaches toward the level of art.

A third reason for the loss of freedom is that there is a tendency to define education—even intelligence—in terms of memory processes, book knowledge, and competence in vocabulary rather than also recognizing the skilled craftsman, musician, artist and athlete as a type of competency. [*Jay B. Nash*]

Responsibilities of Free Men. Because we of this Church are charged with the responsibility and obligation to carry the gospel message to all men, everywhere, we must be deeply concerned—not only with the preservation of freedom throughout the world, but with the restoration of freedom to those who have had it taken away from them, and also with those who have never known what it means to be free. [*Harvey L. Taylor*]

. . . The greatest enemy within our gates today is our own attitude of indifference and complacency. Knowing this, some foreign countries do not hesitate to capitalize on this, our greatest national weakness. We tend to accept our freedom of speech, and our liberty to go and come as we please, as a matter of course. Unless we awaken ourselves to the defense of this privilege, we shall continue to have forces among us that will try to eat out from under us the cornerstone of this freedom and leave us dangling in the air of national disunity. [*Harvey L. Taylor*]

. . . I hold [these four ideas] to be true and significant:

First, that God has bounteously blessed us as a nation and as individuals that we may be free, through the establishment of this republic and the great constitution upon which it rests and through the restoration of the gospel of Jesus Christ.

Secondly, that the blessing of freedom, nationally and individually, is conditional, and that the conditions for national and individual freedom are basically the same; they are personal integrity and righteousness and the achieving of a high moral and religious plane in our personal and our community conduct.

Thirdly, that the conditions imposed by God upon us, upon which our continued national and personal freedom depend, are not being met and that, therefore, as a nation and as individuals, we are in trouble.

And finally, that we as individuals have the responsibility to stand steady in our great heritage, earning anew individually and thus possessing personally the great virtues and truths our fathers made available to us. If we do this we may expect God's continued blessing in keeping us free personally and as a nation. [*Marion D. Hanks* 1]

Obedience and Freedom. In this university, [BYU] I hope that you are learning the truth, that you can recognize it when you hear it and that you are willing to embrace the truth in all fields of learning. You must realize that there are laws which govern our physical existence, and laws which govern our spiritual growth; and when you disobey a law, you have lost a freedom, for the consequences of breaking the law are upon you and curtail you in your happiness. He only is free who has learned to obey all laws. There is no freedom apart from education, apart from learning. [*William E. Berrett*]

Tolerance and Freedom.   . . . as you strive to increase in favor with man, be ever on your guard that you do not, unwittingly, in the name of tolerance, broadmindedness, and so-called liberalism, encourage foreign "isms" and unsound theories which strike at the very root of all we hold dear in America, including our faith in God. Proposals will be offered and programs will be sponsored that have wide, so-called "humanitarian" appeal. Attractive labels are usually attached to the most dangerous programs, often in the name of public welfare and personal security. Have the courage to apply this standard of truth: Determine what the effect of the various issues at stake is upon the character, the integrity, and freedom of man. Which increase his freedom? Which abrogate or destroy? Which recognize and respect the individual dignity of man? [*Ezra Taft Benson* 3]

Road to Freedom. If we would be free we must do more than live in a land that proclaims freedom. We must follow the road to freedom. The road is plain; it has been marked out by the Savior of all men. There are four important requirements: First, you must learn the truth, concerning God, and the purpose of your life. Second, you must become master of your own body. Third, you must learn to love both God and man. And fourth, you must gain a testimony of the living God. This is the road to freedom. This is the road taught by Jesus, who found his people in political bondage—people who sought to have him raise armies that they might strike off the Roman yoke, but he said rather to them: "Ye shall know the truth, and the truth shall make you free." [*William E. Berrett*]

Security and Freedom. We have a classic example of the loss of economic freedom by the misuse of free agency in the book of Genesis. The Egyptians, instead of exercising their agency to provide for themselves against a day of need, depended upon the government. As a result, when the famine came they were forced to purchase food from the government. First, they used their money. When that was gone they gave their livestock; then their lands; and finally they were compelled to sell themselves into economic slavery that they might eat.

We Americans have gone a long way down this road. ourselves during the last quarter of a century. I counsel you students to beware of the doctrine which encourages you to seek government-supported security rather than opportunity and faith in your own industry. [*Marion G. Romney* 2]

Gambling

. . . I warn all of you against gambling. Gambling is not a fair exchange of values, and it breeds a deadly disease which not only jeopardizes business careers, but also brings to its victims, their innocent families and others, disgrace and stigma from which frequently they never recover. I wish I had the time to tell you of specific cases which have come under my observation which I could hope might be a deterrent against any of you ever indulging in this treacherous practice. Stealing, divorce, family disgrace, and even suicide are not uncommonly the final results of betting and putting the first nickel in the slot machine. Avoid it as you would a plague. [*Stephen L Richards* 3]

Godhead

Knowing God.

And this is life eternal, that they might know thee the only true God, and Jesus Christ, whom thou hast sent. (John 17:3.)

We now see how priceless is a true knowledge and understanding of God. If we are to attribute any meaning to this wonderful passage of scripture, we must concede at the very outset of our pursuit for wisdom that God is comprehensible. We can and do know and understand him. The evidence is at hand—ready for us to study and to consider. The desire to know is inherent within us. [*Henry D. Moyle* 4]

Achieving Godhood. The idea of our divine origin, the purpose and possible destiny of man, should inspire intelligent and reverent facing of life's experiences. . . . Religion should be a vital part of everything we think and do. An understanding of God and man's relationship to him should inspire us, in humility, to dare to say, "As God is, man may become." Even though the difference between us is inestimably great, it is one of degree rather than of kind. Given time, with God as a teacher, and with his love in the relationship of Father and Son, there is no limit to what man may accomplish. [*Hugh B. Brown* 5]

Importance of Understanding Our Relationship to God.

Having a Perfect Person as an ideal, inspires hope in eventual self-fulfillment, in the possibility of becoming a perfect person. This God-image quality of man's nature is the very root of his dignity. There is a spark in man which is not found in any other of God's creations, and if we are going to utilize and bring to fruition that holy spark, we as individuals must come to have personal concepts with relation to God and some understanding of our relationship of him. [*Hugh B. Brown* 5]

Personality of God. Out of all these experiences, and many others, we are given a true picture of his [God's] stature. We definitely learn of his personality. We are taught that God is omnipotent, omniscient, that his influence is omnipresent, that he personifies kindness, benevolence, loving tenderness; he is long-suffering, patient, merciful. He is at the same time firm and jealous in his purpose to save his children from destruction here upon the earth. He is the author of our existence. [*Henry D. Moyle* 4]

Government

Divine Approval of the Constitution. . . . to me the Constitution of the United States is a part of my religion; it has become so because of the words of the Lord which I have read to you. [D. & C. 98:4-8, 101:76-80.] So far as I know, he has never given an approval such as this to any other government in the world. So far as I can see, the Constitution of the United States, as of 1833, was his plan of government, reserving and guaranteeing these great rights which you must enjoy if you are going to remain free, if you are going to worship as you wish, if you are going to be a free people. [*J. Reuben Clark, Jr.* 6]

Principle and Government. The greatest lesson to be drawn from the crucifixion is that principles are more to be valued than life itself. Our Savior was willing to suffer physical pain and indignity and give his life for a principle. Peter was willing to fight for his Master's life, but he had a hard time comprehending the purpose of the Master in going to the cross without a fight. The Master's willingness to die for us is more important than anything else in life—this lesson is more important than any other respecting governments or political institutions. [*Ernest L. Wilkinson* 2]

U. S. Constitution. We must be eternally vigilant to see that our form of government is preserved in essentially the form our forefathers intended. Some of our political thinkers, parading under the false cloak of so-called modern liberalism, by continually enlarging the power of the executive branch of our government at the expense of our Judiciary and by the sacrifice of human rights, would take this nation down the alien and treacherous road of concentration of power in the direction of a great Sanhedrin. We have already gone so far in this direction that hundreds of matters are decided by the administrative tribunals and never reach courts for decisions. These tribunals very often act as prosecutor, judge, and jury in defiance of the spirit of our Constitution. [*Ernest L. Wilkinson* 2]

Tests of Government Services.   I have often said there are *three tests* we ought to apply when we are considering asking our great federal government to perform any service for us as taxpayers, as citizens, as members of this government. First of all, assuming that the service is needed, *can the government do it more efficiently than it can be done locally or on a state level or by some private agency?* Generally speaking, the services rendered by the federal government are not highly efficient. There is no profit motive. There is no competition. These are the very life of business. The absence of these tends toward inefficiency.

Secondly, how will it affect our free institutions, our local governments, the home, the school, the church and our other institutions?

Thirdly, I think we should ask the question, how will it affect the morale and the character of the people if this or that service is performed by the central government?

In other words, I think we should take a searching look at this question of freedom today and whether or not we are tending to weaken our hold on it.

We should recognize that the Founding Fathers did not invent this priceless boon of individual freedom and respect for the dignity of man. That great gift to mankind sprang from the Creator and not from government. But the Founding Fathers with superb genius, I believe, welded together certain safeguards which we must always protect to the very limit if we would preserve and strengthen the blessings of freedom.

They found it necessary to turn to religion and to the scriptures in order to have their new experiments make sense. But they were guided by allegiance to basic principles. These principles must be kept in mind always by those of us who are here today and reaping the benefits and the blessings which they so wisely provided. We must be careful that we do not trade freedom for security. Whenever that is attempted, usually we lose both. There is always a tendency when nations become mature for the people to become more interested in preserving their luxuries and their comforts than in safeguarding the ideals and principles which made these comforts and luxuries possible. [*Ezra Taft Benson* 2]

Increasing Government Power. In 1921 or thereabouts, there was quite a depression in the land, and up in Rich County, Utah, we found that we could not open the school unless the company paid its taxes. In Rich County we had no railroads or public utilities or big taxpayers—we were all livestockmen. The individuals were not able to borrow, and could not pay their taxes. And we appealed to the company, to borrow money to pay its taxes, and that it did.

The interesting thing was a meeting held in the little county courthouse in Randolf, where principal citizens from each precinct in the county gathered, together with the county commissioners and the board of education, to fix the budget for the coming year. When it came to fixing the budget for roads, one good brother spoke up . . . and said, "I have a team of horses and a grader. I'm willing to keep the roads in my precinct open good enough for me to travel on, and until we get more money, the stranger within our gates will have to be satisfied with them too." And so, in turn, those private citizens committed themselves to maintain the roads within their various precincts in that county. The county road budget was nil.

The sheriff wanted a deputy, so one man spoke up and said, "Well, I have two able-bodied sons. When you need a deputy, call on me and I'll have one of my sons or both of them, respond gratuitously."

In 1930 the same situation arose. That same county undertook to do that same thing, and what happened? There was a body in the state capitol that had been invested, in the meantime, with the power to regulate the affairs of the local counties. When the county undertook to follow that same pattern, the state body said no, you can't do it, you must levy two or three mills for your roads, and so forth. And we became conscious, in a very practical and emphatic sort of way, that we had lost a liberty: the right of local self-government in Rich County, during that interval. [*Henry D. Moyle* 1]

Gratitude

I have suggested that in the experience of real gratitude there are at least two elements present: there is a vivid awareness of blessings received; there is also the feeling that the blessings received are something *given* to us, not something that we have *earned*. Gratitude is, therefore, an experience deeply felt. It is something that cannot be expressed in the mere language of good manners, in the casual "thank you's" of social relations. Our polite words are frequently just bread expediently cast on the social waters, certain to return to us in a profitable reputation for gentility. Genuine gratitude comes to us only in memorable moments, moments when we know that we are in possession of life's most precious things, and when we also know, with deep humility, that we are quite unworthy of them. To know such moments is to know gratefulness in depth. It is to know one of the most chastening, and at the same time one of the most sustaining experiences of life. [*Parley A. Christensen*]

Gratitude that has depth humbles us. But it also lifts and sustains us. In the presence of the world's unaccountable goodness, the world's unaccountable tragedy is somehow softened. The worst seems endurable to us when all about us stand our friends and loved ones radiating a goodness that asks no questions about our deserts, that refuses to balance our mistakes, our sins, on the cold scales of retributive justice, but rather offers its healing and redemptive blessings according to our needs. The theologies, the logic, of men may dictate retributive justice. The hearts of good men dictate creative justice, the justice that looks beyond what we are to what through repentance and forgiveness we may become. Gratitude in the dimension of depth teaches us that good men and women are often in their human relations superior to the principles they profess; they are frequently better than the creeds to which they subscribe. [*Parley A. Christensen*]

Home and Family

Importance of the Home. No nation can rise above its homes. In building character, the church, the school, and even the nation, stand helpless when confronted with a weakened and degraded home. The good home is the rock foundation—the cornerstone of civilization. There can be no genuine happiness separate and apart from a good home, with the old-fashioned virtues at its base. If this, our nation, is to endure, the home must be safeguarded, strengthened and restored to its rightful importance.

The foundation of a happy home must be laid during pre-marital days. The young people concerned should keep their relationships on a happy, but high plane. Moral purity is an eternal principle. Its violation destroys the noblest qualities and aspirations of man. Purity is life-giving; unchastity is deadly.

There is grave danger in loose and promiscuous relations of young people. The harmful effects of unseemly familiarities are carried over into married life, bringing disappointment, heartache and the weakening of the structure of the home. Unchastity is the most damning of all evils, while moral purity is one of the greatest bulwarks of successful homemaking. Happy and successful homes—let alone individual lives—cannot be built on immorality.

Guard your virtue as you would guard your lives. Reserve for the marriage relationship the sweet and soul-satisfying intimacies of life. The God of Heaven, who instituted the marriage covenant, so intended. He has commanded purity of life and a single standard for men and women. If you fail as young people to properly restrain yourselves, you will pay the penalty in heartache, disappointment and loss of self-respect. Do not reach out too eagerly for the excitements and thrills of life, or they will turn to ashes in your hands. They will come in their own due time in the sacred bonds of marriage.

Youthful sweethearts, be true to God's holy laws. Remember, they cannot be broken with impunity. If you would be happy and successful in your early association, courtship and home-building, conform your lives to the eternal laws of heaven. There is no other way.

Marriage, designed to be an eternal covenant, is the most glorious and most exalting principle ordained for the mature development of man. It has the greatest capacity to develop to the fullest the positive virtues of life—unselfishness, tenderness, compassion, love, devotion, integrity, honesty, service, purity, nobility, and a host of others. No ordinance is of more importance and none more sacred and more necessary to the eternal joy of man. Faithfulness to the marriage covenant brings the fullest joy here and glorious rewards hereafter. The abuse of this sacred ordinance despoils the lives of individuals, wrecks the basic institution of the home and causes the downfall of nations. [*Ezra Taft Benson* 3]

The Home As a Missionary. I was over in Seoul in Korea recently, and one of the finest men we have over in that country is a man by the name of Dr. Ho Jik Kim. He is a graduate from Cornell University with a doctor's degree. He has returned to his native land now as an advisor to the Korean government. He is a leader of one of the educational institutions there, and around him he has gathered now thirty-four converts, many of them well-educated. We talked with him for some two hours, trying to lay a foundation that might establish itself into a beginning of missionary activities in the land of Korea. He told us about his conversion.

"The thing that attracted me to the Church," he explained, "was when I was invited into the homes of two Latter-day Saint men who were on the faculty of Cornell University. The thing that I was most impressed by was the kind of home life they had. I never had been in homes where there was such a sweet relationship between husband and wife, and father and mother and children. I had seen them engage in family prayer. I was so impressed that I began to inquire about this religion of theirs. And one night after I had studied for a long time and had become convinced about the desirability of belonging to such a company, I knew first I must get a testimony. I went down on my knees and prayed nearly all night long and I received a testimony of the divinity of this work." But remember it all started because of the excellent example of a family that lived the kind of home life that the gospel expects of true Latter-day Saints. [*Harold B. Lee* 3]

The Family An Eternal Organization. . . . outside of the celestial kingdom there will be found no family organization. We should remember that these privileges of associating as families eternally are reserved for those who are willing to abide every covenant and every obligation which we are called upon to receive while we sojourn here upon the earth. [*ElRay L. Christiansen* 1]

Importance of Gospel Teaching in the Home. I appreciate President Wilkinson's reference to my father. You know, I was reared in a very unusual home. Because of certain conditions which arose, as he stated, my father was released from the Quorum of the Twelve Apostles. He was not disfellowshipped; he was not excommunicated, but he had to hold his priesthood in abeyance for a number of years, until the First Presidency again gave him the green light to go ahead. I suppose he was officially inactive for some twenty-seven or twenty-eight years. At the beginning of that period his children were mostly young. I was just seven or eight years of age. He couldn't officiate in the priesthood in any

way. But they couldn't stop him from being the patriarch
of his own family, from presiding in his own home. And I
wouldn't be here today, fellow students, if it had not been
for the integrity and the devotion and the loyalty of my
father to the Church of Jesus Christ of Latter-day Saints.
During those years of his inactivity, he kept his sons on
missions for twenty-five years, three of us in the islands of
the seas, one in Australia and two in Europe, in Germany.
When I think of my father . . . I think of the last words of
King George's Christmas Broadcast in 1939. I listened to
that broadcast in New Zealand. Britain was then in the
war. And at the end of his broadcast he quoted (if I can
remember them) these words:

> I said to the man who stood at the gate of the year
> 'Give me a light that I may tread safely into the unknown.'
> And he replied, 'Go out into the darkness and put your
> hand into the hand of God. That is better than light and
> safer than a known way.'

During these years in our home when there was con-
siderable darkness of disappointment, my father never hesi-
tated to place his hand in the hand of God. And that indeed
was to him better than a light and better than the known
way. He taught us to pray. And that was his way, his
medium of bearing his testimony to us and of instructing
us while he was upon his knees in prayer. Each of us took
his turn, but it seemed that Father's turn came around often-
er and he was one of the longest prayers I have ever heard.
I think more than once when he said, "Amen," I wasn't
even in the room. I was pretty fast crawling on my knees.
But in his prayers he always poured out his heart to God,
and always pleaded with him, not necessarily for himself,
but for his children, his family. And I don't think he ever
offered up a prayer, but what in that prayer there was this
petition, "Holy Father, if there ever comes a time when my
children have to choose between following me, their father,
or being loyal and devoted to thy holy priesthood, please

give to them the courage and the fortitude to forsake their own father and be loyal to the priesthood which thou hast restored to the earth." No sermon has ever impressed me more than those words in his prayer. My, how fathers can save their families by remaining true and loyal regardless of circumstances and disappointments.

There came a time in my life when I decided I would get married. I was then attending school in Washington, and I made plans with my sweetheart—she is the one I married. I rushed her so fast she couldn't send me a "Dear John" letter. But I was struggling to earn my way in Washington, to get an education and I didn't have enough money to come and get married in the temple. So we made plans to get married in New York, and then when I finished school we were to come home and be sealed in the temple. We even had the announcements printed, and then all of a sudden my father heard about it. Now I know what he did. He wasn't a man of means. He was never successful in a business way, and I guess things looked pretty dark for him as far as I was concerned. So he went out and put his hand into the hand of God. I know he did it on his knees, and in response to that prayer, I received money from him, and he said, "You have to come home and get married right in the first instance."

I came home and we went to the temple. I will never forget that morning. It was the 13th of July. But that morning we met at the temple, my father and my mother, some of our family. We came around from West Temple where we lived, just across the street from the temple block. My wife and her family came and we met at that little gate at the east wall of the temple. There we met and went in, all but my father. He couldn't go beyond that little gate. And yet I was going in there because of him, because of his faith, his devotion, his integrity, because he had as the greatest obsession of his life, the salvation of his children. I'll never forget that picture.

My, the good he did during those years of inactivity. You know, my father never used to say, "Come on, boys, let's go to meeting." He would always say, "Let's go and partake of the sacrament." Yes, he could partake of the sacrament, but he couldn't bless it. He could do almost anything a woman could do in the Church except go to the temple. And so we would go and partake of the sacrament, and I learned from him the importance of that sacred right, that here in the sacrament meeting, before the sacrament board, we could renew our covenants and keep them in force. We could learn that the young priest in his tender years, as President Joseph Fielding Smith so beautifully explained recently, could place us all under covenant. Yes, the young priest can place everyone under covenant, even up to and including the Prophet, Seer, and Revelator of the Church. So I learned to go and partake of the sacrament.

Then I was called on a mission. Oh, my father always saw to it that the boys were called on missions. They didn't used to screen them in those days like they do now. The bishop would just look around and see what was going on, and then he would say, "Oh, oh, there's young Cowley. We'd better get him out in the mission field, and get him there quick." So out we'd go, three of us at the age of seventeen. And I will never forget the prayers of my father the day that I left. I have never had a more beautiful blessing in all my life. Then his last words to me at the railroad station, "My boy, you will go out on that mission; you will study; you will try to prepare your sermons, and sometimes when you are called upon you will think you are wonderfully prepared, but when you stand up, your mind will go completely blank." I have had that experience more than once.

I said, "What do you do when your mind goes blank?"

He said, "You stand up there and with all the fervor of your soul, you bear witness that Joseph Smith was a

Prophet of the living God, and thoughts will flood into your mind and words to your mouth, to round out those thoughts in a facility of expression that will carry conviction to the heart of everyone who listens." And so my mind, being mostly blank during my five years in the mission field, gave me the opportunity to bear testimony to the greatest event in the history of the world since the crucifixion of the Master. Try it sometime. . . . If you don't have anything else to say, testify that Joseph Smith was the Prophet of God, and the whole history of the Church will flood into your mind, the principles of the gospel, faith, repentance, baptism, the laying on of hands for the gift of the Holy Ghost, tithing—ten percent—fasting, the honest cost of a meal as a contribution. All these things will flood into your mind, if you will but bear testimony that the Prophet was indeed a servant of God and an instrument in his hands. It is wonderful to retain in your minds the lessons you get in your homes. [*Matthew Cowley* 3]

Honesty

I believe that honesty is so much a part of the Gospel of Christ that we cannot escape it. No matter how many times we go to church and no matter how many times we get on our knees and pray, no matter how much money we might pay as tithing or offerings, if we are not honest about it then we are as tinkling cymbals and sounding brass. Honesty is fundamental to good character. Honesty is fundamental in the Gospel of the Lord, Jesus Christ. And that honesty must apply to every phase of our lives. It must not only have to do with our money and such things as that, but it should also touch every part of our lives. [*Mark E. Petersen* 5]

Jesus Christ

A Complete Concept of Christ. I sometimes wonder whether our concept of the Christ is not somewhat circumscribed
within the limits of his mortal service. We think of him as
the lowly Carpenter, living in a lowly home, going through
his life mission, befriended sometimes, scoffed and scorned
at at other times, and finally, crucified by his own. We read
of his miracles, we read of his great teachings, the great
truths which he gave to us, but we think of him very largely
as a mortal being. Some may judge his Messiahship by his
mortal service. This service, properly understood, will give
the true picture; but too often there is incomplete understanding.

We might begin by recalling that Christ is the First-
born of the Father; the Only Begotten of the Father (and
we add according to the flesh). He sits on the right hand
of the Father. He acts for and in behalf of the Father, as
an agent of the Father "to reign with almighty power
according to the will of the Father." [*J. Reuben Clark, Jr.* 1]

Jesus as the Redeemer. I am only wanting to point out
that in many respects his [Jesus Christ's] teachings were
known, his miracles had been duplicated before; some of
them were duplicated after by the Apostles who lived after
him. They have been and are duplicated in our day. That
was not his distinctive work. He came here; he restored the
gospel; he fulfilled the law of Moses; he did away with sacrifice; he declared to the people on this continent that
thereafter their sacrifice was to be "a broken heart and a

contrite spirit." (III Nephi 9:20.) He lived, he died, was crucified, lay in the tomb, was resurrected, and by that act of sacrifice he made certain that every man and woman born to this earth will be resurrected. This was his work as Redeemer. [*J. Reuben Clark, Jr.* 5]

Reverence for Christ. Christ is the only "name under heaven given among men, whereby we must be saved." Nearly two thousand years have gone and today he is acknowledged among the sincere people as the one peerless person among all mankind, but not among all as divine.

Wherein lies his greatness? We do not honor him as a great discoverer; we do not worship him as a scientist, as a literary genius, nor as one noted in the realm of art, nor as one distingushed in the realm of invention, in statesmanship or war. In fact, in none of the realms in which men and women of the world have won their laurels do we pay deference to Jesus. We revere him because of his wisdom and spirituality which exceed that of all other men who ever lived, and above all that, we revere, we worship him as our God. [*David O. McKay* 2]

Value of Christ's Teachings. I say to you that there is more virtue and power in the simple teachings of Christ than contained in all the philosophies of men. His teachings will do more to produce proper attitudes, beautiful character, true principles of service, and will also give more purpose to life with a full measure of joy and happiness to each of you, than any other teachings can. [*Delbert L. Stapley* 1]

The Savior of Mankind. I think many times of the suffering of our Savior. I can't understand just how he could take upon himself the burden of our sins to pay the debt, for it was paying a debt; but I accept it on faith. I know that he died that we might live. He died to redeem all men from the grave, and he died to redeem all men from their sins on condition of their repentance and acceptance of his truth. [*Joseph Fielding Smith* 3]

Bedrock of Spirituality. The one infallible guide for men and nations is the life, and the teachings, of Jesus Christ. To understand him and to accept his leadership without reservations is the very bedrock of spirituality. Jesus inferred this when he said: "And this is life eternal, that they might know thee, the only true God, and Jesus Christ, whom thou hast sent." (John 17:3.)

I . . . wrote down a dozen statements about the Master which I felt I could make about no other character in history. I present them to you as follows:

First, Jesus is the only perfect character who has lived upon the earth.

Second, he never made a mistake in his teachings.

Third, he was never confused nor puzzled.

Fourth, he never argued nor contended to establish his point, yet he was the world's greatest teacher.

Fifth, he was the best storyteller of whom we have any record. "The story of the Prodigal Son," said Charles Dickens, "is the most beautiful story in all literature." (See Luke 15:11-22.) There is another one, much like it; I refer to the story of the Good Samaritan, told by Jesus in answer to a question propounded by a "certain lawyer who stood up" and asked, "What shall I do to inherit eternal life?"

"How readest thou?" asked Jesus.

And the lawyer, well versed, said, "Thou shalt love the Lord, thy God, with all thy heart, and with all thy soul, and with all thy strength, and with all thy mind; and thy neighbor as thyself."

Jesus replied promptly, "Thou hast answered right."

But the lawyer was not so easily satisfied. He asked another question. It was a good question too. "Who is my neighbor?"

Jesus answered the question by telling the story of the Good Samaritan. (See Luke 10:25-37.) May I suggest that you read that story, also one which begins, "A sower went out to sow." (See Matt. 13:1-23.) These stories, called parables, were given to remind people of their delinquencies and shortcomings. They went straight to the heart.

The sixth statement reads: He is the most commanding personality in human history. Pilate was uneasy and disturbed before him. Nicodemus appeared stupid in his presence. The Roman soldiers, who came to arrest him in the Garden of Gethsemane, bowed in silent tribute before the majesty of his personality.

Seventh, he met every situation perfectly. He said and did the right thing on every occasion. For example, there is the circumstance of the woman taken in sin. It is not difficult to picture this woman, who had been robbed of the higher instincts of her soul, before the burly men who stood ready to stone her to death. Her case was submitted to Jesus as a challenge. Should not this woman, who was taken in sin be stoned? Jesus knelt down and began to write in the sand. Finally he turned to them and said: "Let him among you who is without sin cast the first stone." These hardened men slunk away, one by one, and soon the woman and Jesus were left alone. Never before was sin so horrible nor purity so pure. I submit to you that on this occasion Jesus gave the perfect answer and conducted himself in the right manner. (See Matt. 8:3-11.)

Eight, he has no parallel as a public speaker. He delivered the greatest sermon ever preached. The Lord's prayer is perfect in its diction. It is comprehensive and complete and covers every phase of humanity's welfare.

Nine, he was terrible in rebuke and administered the most scathing denunciation on record. May I ask you to read at your first opportunity the twenty-third chapter of Matthew where he denounces the religious leaders of the time, the scribes and Pharisees, because of their insincerity and hypocrisy.

Ten, he was the world's most lovable character and yet he made the greatest pretensions.

Eleven, he selected the world's greatest leadership out of the ranks of common men. These men went forth as humble missionaries, but their work and their words lived on after them. Their testimonies changed the course of human history.

Twelve, his character is immaculate, his judgment infallible, his knowledge all-comprehending and his wisdom supreme.

Thirteen, he made love the basis of all human relationships. [*Alma Sonne*]

The Trial of Jesus.   Here, [in the trial of Jesus] in what should have been the greatest trial in all history, no evidence was presented. Jesus was not even permitted to plead truth as a defense. Instead of looking into the truthfulness of his claim that he was the Son of God, which was the charge of blasphemy put into issue, it was assumed that he was not the Son of God. Jesus, therefore, stood convicted of the most heinous offense known in Jewry, all within the space of a few moments. If, in fact, Jesus were not the Son of God, he would have been guilty of blasphemy. If, in fact, Jesus was the Son of God, he was not guilty of blasphemy. If the learned priests who comprised the Sanhedrin had compared the teachings and prophecies of the Old Testament with the events in the life of Jesus, they would have found in fact that he was the Son of God. They would have known that in fulfillment of ancient prophecy he was the Messiah born in Bethlehem of a virgin; that he sprang from the House of David; that he began to preach in Galilee; that he performed many miracles; that he made his public entry into Jerusalem riding upon an ass; and that he should be betrayed by one of his followers for thirty pieces of silver, which would finally be thrown into the potter's field. These, and many other prophecies of the Old Testament, they would have realized had been fulfilled in the life of the Savior.

But no such evidence was examined. On the contrary, in defiance of the most rigid principles of the Jewish Law, that no witness could testify against himself, and that no one could be convicted except upon the sworn, agreed testimony of at least two witnesses, the council resolved that he was a blasphemer. [*Ernest L. Wilkinson* 2]

Joseph Smith

The Prophet's Place in the Gospel Plan. It was Joseph
Smith who saw the visions; it was he who translated the
sacred record and gave us the Book of Mormon. He dic-
tated the revelations found in the Doctrine and Covenants.
He organized the Church and sent out the first missionaries,
all under divine direction. In fact, it seems to me that all
we have and are as a people we owe to that young man;
and yet, he labored all the while in poverty and distress,
among false brethren, and was surrounded by enemies who
persecuted and imprisoned him and finally took his life.
[*Preston Nibley*]

Profile of a Prophet. I should like to be for a few minutes
a witness in support of the proposition that the gospel of
Jesus Christ has been restored in our day and that this is
his Church which was organized under his direction through
the Prophet Joseph Smith. I should like to give some reasons
for the faith I have and for my allegiance to the Church.
Perhaps I can do this more quickly by referring to an interview I had in London, England, in 1939, just before the
outbreak of World War II. I had met a very prominent
English gentleman, a member of the House of Commons,
formerly one of the justices of the Supreme Court of England. In my conversations with this gentleman on various
subjects, "vexations of the soul" he called them, we talked
about business and law, about politics, international relations and war, and we frequently discussed religion. He
called me on the phone one day and asked if I would meet

him at his office and explain some phases of the gospel. He said, "I think there is going to be a war. If there is you will have to return to America and we may not meet again." His statement regarding the imminence of war and the possibility that we would not meet again proved to be prophetic.

When I went to his office he said he was intrigued by some things I had told him. He asked me to prepare a brief on Mormonsim . . . and discuss it with him as I would discuss a legal problem. He said, "You have told me that you believe that Joseph Smith was a prophet. You have said to me that you believe that God the Father and Jesus of Nazareth appeared to Joseph Smith. I cannot understand how a barrister and solicitor from Canada, a man trained in logic and evidence could accept such absurd statements. What you tell me about Joseph Smith seems fantastic, but I think you should take three days at least to prepare a brief and permit me to examine it and question you on it."

I suggested that we proceed at once and have an Examination for Discovery, which is, briefly, a meeting of the opposing sides in a law suit where the plaintiff and defendant, with their attorneys, meet to examine each other's claims and see if they can find some area of agreement, thus saving the time of the court later on. I said perhaps we could see whether we had some common ground from which we could discuss my "fantastic ideas." He agreed to that quite readily.

I can only give you, in the few minutes at my disposal, a condensed and abbreviated synopsis of the three-hour conversation which followed. In the interest of time I shall resort to the question and answer method rather than narration. I began by asking, "May I proceed, sir, on the assumption that you are a Christian?"

"I am."

"I assume you believe in the Bible—the Old and the New Testament?"

"I do!"

"Do you believe in prayer?"

"I do!"

"You say that my belief that God spoke to a man in this age is fantastic and absurd?"

"To me, it is."

"Do you believe that God ever did speak to anyone?"

"Certainly, all through the Bible we have evidence of that."

"Did he speak to Adam?"

"Yes."

"To Enoch, Noah, Abraham, Moses, Jacob, and on through the prophets?"

"I believe he spoke to each of them."

"Do you believe that contact between God and man ceased when Jesus appeared on the earth?"

"No, such communication reached its climax, its apex at that time."

"Do you believe that Jesus was the Son of God?"

"He was."

"Do you believe, sir, that after Jesus was resurrected a certain lawyer, who was also a tentmaker by the name of Saul of Tarsus, when on his way to Damascus, talked with Jesus of Nazareth, who had been crucified, resurrected and had ascended into heaven?"

"I do."

"Whose voice did Saul hear?"

"It was the voice of Jesus Christ for he so introduced himself."

"Then, my Lord, (that is the way we address judges in the British Comonwealth), my Lord, I am submitting to you in all seriousness that it was standard procedure in Bible times for God to talk to man."

"I think I will admit that, but it stopped shortly after the first century of the Christian era."

"Why do you think it stopped?"

"I can't say."

"You think that God hasn't spoken since then?"

"I am sure he hasn't."

"There must be a reason; can you give me a reason?"

"I do not know."

"May I suggest some possible reasons: Perhaps God does not speak to man anymore because he cannot. He has lost the power."

He said, "Of course that would be blasphemous."

"Well, then if you don't accept that, perhaps he doesn't speak to men because he doesn't love us anymore. He is no longer interested in the affairs of men."

"No," he said, "God loves all men, and he is no respecter of persons."

"Well, then, if he could speak, and if he loves us, then the only other possible answer as I see it is that we don't need him. We have made such rapid strides in science, we are so well educated, that we don't need God anymore."

And then he said, and his voice trembled as he thought of impending war, "Mr. Brown, there never was a time in the history of the world when the voice of God was needed as it is needed now. Perhaps you can tell me why he doesn't speak."

My answer was, "He does speak; he has spoken, but men need faith to hear him."

Then we proceeded to prepare what I may call a "profile of a prophet."

* * *

We agreed, between us, that the following characteristics should distinguish a man who claims to be a prophet.

A. He will boldly claim that God had spoken to him.

B. Any man so claiming would be a dignified man with a dignified message; no table-jumping, no whisperings from the dead, no clairvoyance, but an intelligent statement of truth.

C. Any man claiming to be a prophet of God would declare his message without any fear, and without making any weak concessions to public opinion.

D. If he were speaking for God he could not make concessions although what he taught would be new and contrary to the accepted teachings of the day. A prophet bears witness to what he has seen and heard and seldom tries to make a case by argument. His message and not himself is important.

E. Such a man would speak in the name of the Lord saying, "Thus said the Lord," as did Moses, Joshua and others.

F. Such a man would predict future events in the name of the Lord and they would come to pass, as did Isaiah and Ezekiel.

G. He would have not only an important message for his time, but often a message for all future time, such as Daniel, Jeremiah and others had.

H. He would have courage and faith, endure persecution and give his life, if need be, for the cause he espoused, such as Peter, James, Paul and others did.

I. Such a man would denounce wickedness fearlessly. He would generally be rejected or persecuted by the people of his time, but later generations and descendants of his persecutors, would build monuments in his honor.

J. He would be able to do superhuman things, things that no man could do without God's help. The consequence or result of his message and work would be convincing evidence of his prophetic calling. "By their fruits ye shall know them."

K. His teachings would be in strict conformity with scripture and his words and his writings would become scripture. "For the prophecy came not in old time by the will of man; but holy men of God spake as they were moved by the Holy Ghost." (II Peter 1:21.)

* * *

I said to my friend, "My Lord, I cannot understand your saying to me that my claims are fantastic. Nor can I understand why Christians who claim to believe in Christ would persecute and put to death a man [Joseph Smith] whose whole purpose was to prove the truth of the things they themselves were declaring, namely that Jesus was the Christ. I could understand their persecuting Joseph if he had said, "I am Christ," or if he had said, "There is no Christ," or if he had said someone else is Christ; then Christians believing in Christ would be justified in opposing him. But what he said was "He whom ye claim to serve, declare I unto you." Paraphrasing what Paul said in Athens, "Whom therefore ye ignorantly worship, him declare I unto you." (Acts 17:23.) Joseph said to the Christians of his day, "You claim to believe in Jesus Christ. I testify that I saw him and I talked to him. He is the Son of God. Why persecute me for that?"

When Joseph came out of the woods he had at least four fundamental truths, and he announced them to the world. First, that the Father and the Son are separate and distinct individuals. Secondly, that the canon of scripture is not complete. Thirdly, that man was created in the bodily image of God. And fourth, the channel between earth and heaven is open and revelation is continuous.

Perhaps some of you are wondering how the judge reacted to our discussion. He sat and listened intently; he asked some very pointed and searching questions and at the end of the period he said, "Mr. Brown, I wonder if your people appreciate the importance of your message; do you?" He said, "If what you have told me is true, it is the greatest message that has come to this earth since the angels announced the birth of Christ."

This was a judge speaking, a great statesman, an intelligent man. He threw out the challenge, "Do you appreciate the import of what you say?" He added: "I wish it were true. I hope it may be true. God knows it ought to be true. I would to God," he said and he wept as he said it, "that some man could appear on earth and authoritatively say, 'Thus saith the Lord.'"

As I intimated, we did not meet again. I have brought to you very briefly some of the reasons why I believe that Joseph Smith was a prophet of God. But undergirding and overarching all that, I say to you from the very center of my heart that by the revelations of the Holy Ghost I know that Joseph Smith was a prophet of God. While these evidences and many others that could be cited may have the effect of giving one an intellectual conviction, only by the whisperings of the Holy Spirit can one come to know the things of God. By those whisperings I say I know that Joseph Smith is a prophet of God. I thank God for that knowledge and pray for his blessings upon all of you in the name of Jesus Christ. Amen. [*Hugh B. Brown* 3]

Joy

. . . I should like to break down briefly the key word used in the famous Mormon statement, "Men are that they might have joy."

The key word as you see is joy, J-O-Y. Joy consists of three parts. The first part is pleasure, which is derived from play—dancing, hunting, fishing, physical games . . . music and the like. Of course, the funful diversions should be clean and healthful. The second part of joy is happiness, which is a by-product of work. To be really happy we must be active in some productive achievement, professional or manual. The happiest person in the world, no doubt, is the mother who is loved by her children and her husband, because she's the hardest worker.

The third part of joy is blessedness, which comes through prayer and the grace of our Father in Heaven, and from being true to our loyalties in the Church. Prayer is a great spiritual dynamic. Prayer will take light to places, for instance, that electricity will never penetrate.

Put these three together now—pleasure from play, happiness from work, and blessedness from prayer, and you have the real meaning of joy. [*Earl J. Glade*]

Law

Limitations of Law. There are certain things that we cannot accomplish by law or by any process of government. We cannot legislate intelligence. We cannot legislate morality. No, and we cannot legislate loyalty, for loyalty is a kind of morality. We cannot produce these things by decrees of commissions or public inquisitions. [*Henry D. Moyle* 5]

Positive Aspects of Law. We are too inclined to think of law as something merely restrictive—something hemming us in. We sometimes think of law as the opposite of liberty. But that is a false conception. That is not the way that God's inspired prophets and lawgivers looked upon the law. Law has a twofold purpose. It is meant to govern. It is also meant to educate. Take for example one of the most ordinary, everyday laws affecting all of us—the traffic regulations. The traffic laws, when they are observed, prevent accidents. They also produce good drivers. That is their educational function. [*Cecile B. DeMille*]

Law versus Tyranny. If man will not be ruled by God, he will certainly be ruled by tyrants—and there is no tyranny more imperious or more devastating than man's own selfishness, without the law. [*Cecil B. DeMille*]

Living Our Religion

Depth of Religious Experience. Some have falsely supposed that a religious life is a life without the experiences of ecstacy in personal living, an existence in self-denial of the soul-stirring, passion-filled, exhilarating experiences of life. Exactly the opposite is true. I bear you my solemn witness that in a deeply religious life founded in the eternal principles of revealed truth, the dynamic creative forces of life, divinely comprehended, expressed in the spirit of sacredness and channeled within the bounds of righteous law, are experienced with an intensity and power intimately integral to God's own power and far surpassing in exquisite rapture anything basically carnal that flesh and blood can produce. [*Lynn A. McKinlay*]

Live Gospel Ideals. If I could express my most heartfelt wish for you, I would say to you, and to young folks everywhere—if you would obtain the highest success and the most contentment of mind, practice in your daily contacts the ideals of the gospel of Jesus Christ. I do not hesitate to make that statement without modifications. I know the results will be what I indicated. They will make you handsomer, young men—more beautiful, young women—because your thoughts modify your features. They may not be the handsomest, but they will radiate that which makes handsome young men and beautiful young women. They will make you more dutiful sons and daughters, more clever students, more faithful lovers, more desirable companions, more loyal friends, more helpful members of society, more worthy mothers and fathers of future families, make you sons and daughters of God more successful in fulfilling the measure of your creation on earth. [*David O. McKay* 4]

Business Pressure versus Maintaining Principle. You will be tempted in many other subtle ways to abandon your principles. For example, you will hear argued that a business deal can better be consummated or personal advantage realized more readily in the cocktail lounge than in the office or in the home. I can testify that in experience in business or in my personal affairs, I have never found it necessary to succumb to such practices in order to maintain position and progress in this competitive world. The din of familiar argument will mount suggesting that you can increase or improve your popularity, your position or your standing by being a good fellow, by going along with the crowd. Don't be misled by this false premise. Inducements, financial and otherwise may well be brandished before you to give testimony or take a stand which you know is contrary to your belief and knowledge. Particularly in communities where LDS people are in the minority, efforts will be made to draw you into the ever accelerating trend to convert the Holy Sabbath Day into a holiday. Be on guard that you are not counted as one giving impetus to this violation of the word of the Lord to his children. Pressure may be exerted upon you to spend hours each month around a card table. Rather than succumbing to such influence use these hours in a constructive pursuit. When your finances are tightest you may expect some to say that you could defer your compliance with the great law of tithing. There were no such exceptions cited when the Lord said in referring to this commandment, "Prove me now herewith if I will not open you the windows of heaven and pour you out a blessing which shall be so great that there will be no room to receive it." (Malachi 3:10.) [*Milan D. Smith*]

Rules for Living. I have taken the Ten Commandments and the Beatitudes and the Articles of Faith and have tried to bring them down to five simple statements:

1. Live in honor. . . .
2. Covet or seize no man's property.
3. Wrong no one's good name.
4. Make a habit of being helpful, of doing some little kindness along the way.
5. Keep in regular contact with your Maker.

[*Adam S. Bennion* 3]

Business Success and Church Standards. Sometimes when I am with Mormons, I am surprised to have them say, "Rose Marie, I think it is wonderful that you have been so successful in business and yet have stayed a good member of the Church."

I think each time I hear it, "That is backwards! It is *because* I am a member of the Church that I have been successful in business. Can't you understand that?"

I often think, when I look at young people who are starting in business, of something Dr. Fletcher said one time when I was in New York at conference. He said, "It is not hard to be a Mormon among non-Mormons. All you have to do is *tell your friends you are a Mormon and they will see to it that you live your religion.*" I really did not realize the tremendous thing that he was saying, until I learned that other people respect us and are proud to know us, and want us *never* to let them down. They want us to live up to our standards.

So, if you want to know the very first and most important thing to do to become a success in business it is this: Tell everyone you meet that you are a Mormon, and then live your religion to the utmost of your ability. As sure as you do, the most wonderful blessings will follow as automatically as day follows night. [*Rose Marie Reid*]

The Importance of Exemplary Living. A few years ago a young man dressed in the military uniform of a lieutenant came into my office just before Christmas and said that he had just been mustered out of service in Denver in time to go back to his home in New York City in time for Christmas. But he had elected to come on to Salt Lake City rather than go home for Christmas and had a letter of introduction to Elder Kimball of the Council of the Twelve from Brother Kimball's relatives whom he had met in Denver. But upon learning that Brother Kimball had gone home, down in Arizona for Christmas, he came to my office as a substitute for a visit with Brother Kimball.

He said to me, "I have come to Salt Lake City rather than to go home in order that I can see how the Mormons celebrate Christmas." What he was saying in effect was, "I'd like to see how the members of the Church which bears the name of Jesus Christ celebrate his birthday." Do you know I had some misgivings about the purpose of this inquiry and his coming, because just before Christmas I have seen long lines of people reaching almost a block long, lined up to get into a certain store, one of which is located on 2nd South and 3rd West in Salt Lake City, a state-controlled liquor business. And I have seen these men drink themselves silly on Christmas to celebrate the birthday of the Lord and Savior of the world. And I wondered if he should come along and see a long line of people going in to buy liquor for that purpose, would he assume that they were all non-members or that they were tourists just passing through, desiring to get a little liquid refreshment?

We outlined his stay which included a visit to the Temple Square where he was to spend some hours. On Sunday morning he was to go and hear the Tabernacle Choir. President McKay was to give the Church of the Air address. That was all perfectly fine. We arranged for him to go up to the Capitol Hill Ward, which is one of our fine wards—beautiful building. And then on Saturday night he called me and said, "Brother Lee, I wonder if you could direct me to a young people's dancing party where members of the Church are at play. I'd like to see how the members of your Church conduct themselves at the dance." Do you know, . . . I had some anxieties about that, because I have watched some of our young people dance and carry on antics on the dance floor that ought to be nowhere but in a circus or on a vaudeville stage.

Well, we got by Saturday all right and I called him anxiously the next afternoon to see if he wouldn't like to come to a fireside. Now in case some of you don't know what a fireside is, it is a place where they gather a group of young people together and choose some victim at which to fire questions. I was the victim that they had chosen this night, some hundred and fifty of these young people. This young man sat there and listened to their questions. One of them asked something like this, "Does this Church know how many of its members have been converted to the gospel from reading the Book of Mormon?"

And, I answered, "Of course, we have no such accounting." But I said I believed that the Book of Mormon is the greatest missionary we have.

And at that this young man raised his hand and said, "May I say something?" And then he stood up and said to these young people. "I'm afraid you young people don't realize the importance of your place as Church members. I have visited many of the great cities of the world. I've come back here with a critical mind to look at you from a close range." He said, "I find you different than people I have found in most cities. I walk up and down your streets and I find less drunkenness; I find less smoking and so on." And he said, "You people are the best missionaries your Church has. It is not your Book of Mormon, as great as that is, and I have read it. But the greatest missionary you have is the individual member of your Church. Now whether you like it or not, you are a missionary, either a bad missionary or a good missionary. It's that which attracts folks like me into the Church." [*Harold B. Lee* 3]

The Power of Example. In one of the European mission homes I met a young missionary who was counselor to the president of the mission. He had been a convert to the Church only a little more than one year when he received his mission call. I asked him how he happened to join the Church. He said he had attended one of the large midwestern universities where he was earning his tuition by selling beer in a tavern. He often watched the boys who came into the place to buy beer. A growing disgust developed within him as he watched so many of the fine, trained young men waste themselves and their time on drinking.

Later he moved to California and enrolled in one of the universities there. One day a young man came into the inn where he was working and invited him to join him in drinking a glass of beer. He said the boy did not look millrun, so he accepted the invitation. He asked the young man what he was doing there. The boy explained that he had come from Utah, that he had been attending the Brigham Young University, but he had left school because of its strict discipline. He told of the ban of the school against smoking and drinking among the students, saying the restrictions were so irksome to him that he had been forced to leave. The young missionary said he thought to himself, "What a wonderful school and how very right they are!" He was so interested in a university that had such standards that he cultivated the companionship of this young man, often going to his room where they played cards.

One day there came into the room a second Latter-day Saint from Brigham Young University to visit his friend. This boy sat and watched the card game, but did not play. He casually explained that it was against his teachings as a Latter-day Saint. The young missionary said he immediately became interested in this boy who lived as he was taught and as he believed. He was intrigued by a Church which had such unusual, yet sound teachings. He determined to learn something of this second boy. He cultivated his friendship which resulted in his conversion to the Church. [*Belle S. Spafford*]

Sunday Religion. An old friend came into my office the other day, and told me how much money he was making in a certain racket, a legalized racket. He called it a racket, and he was embarrassed by the fact that he was making so much money so easily and was high pressuring and duping so many people. . . .

He said, "You know, I learned long ago that you can't mix religion and economics. And so to keep my life in balance, I work forty hours a week in business and I've taken on a new interest in Church work." That kind of a balanced life is not going to bring peace to his community.

Let me give you another illustration of what a devoted church worker did. A certain lawyer and this man learned, some years ago, on good authority, that the government was going to buy property in a certain area to build a plant. These men went around to buy up all the property. They offered a good widow, of my acquaintance, $200 an acre for her land, for which she had only paid $40 an acre some twenty years back. They explained to her that the land probably would never have too much value, that they were gambling and that it was a good sale for her. They knew that if the government bought that property it would be worth $1000 an acre, and they were very sure the government would do that. And so they went ahead and bought the property from this widow for $200 an acre. They didn't explain that risk to her; they didn't explain their purpose. She found out afterward. And these men are good, ardent church workers and do a very nice job—inside the building. [*Lowell L. Bennion*]

Abandoning Church Standards to Gain Favor.   I shall never forget when I sat as a member of the Salt Lake City Commission. We were in a budget session. We had been smoked out for hours and hours and hours in this grueling experience which was new to me. Three of the men in the group were inveterate smokers and as we began to relax as it neared the lunch period they began to exchange stories; the mayor was a Jew and one of the others was an Irishman. And so they began to tell Jewish and Irish stories. They were pretty good, sometimes tinged a little at the end.

There came in one of our officers, whose name I will not reveal, just to hear the end of one of these stories; and thinking apparently to win the applause of the commission, he told one of the filthiest, rottenest stories that I think I have ever listened to. There wasn't much laughter and he retired shortly. Then one of the commissioners, not a member of the Church, in fact quite critical sometimes, turned to me and said, "There is one of your damn Mormon bishops." How the stock of the Church went down! What a disgrace to think that a man who had been a bishop in this Church would so forget himself as to allow the levity and the filthiness of an unclean mind to express itself in the hope of some kind of personal acclaim! [*Harold B. Lee* 3]

Testimony of One Who Has Been Excommunicated.   The other day there came to my office a man who a few years ago was excommunicated from the Church because of a very serious transgression. After these years of sad, humiliating, tragic experience, he is wondering how he can find his way back into the Church. Well, you might ask me, "Why should he have been excommunicated?" The more we give to a person in this Church, the more the Lord expects of him. We wouldn't baptize an individual unless we were assured that that individual was repentant of his sins. We wouldn't think of conferring the Holy Ghost upon him unless we felt that he was prepared to receive it. We wouldn't give to him the Holy Priesthood which would only be a burden he was not prepared to carry . . . unless we thought he was worthy of it. And so it is when one has sinned so seriously that to hold further membership or to hold the Holy Priesthood would be as a stumbling block and a burden rather than a blessing; in the wisdom of the Lord, these privileges are taken from him that he might be ground as "clay in the hands of the potter," again tried and tested until after that testing he is worthy again to receive these holy blessings.

This man had been excommunicated. He was sitting in a stake conference a few weeks ago. One of the general authorities was there and was talking about some of these matters. The general authority said, "One of the most terrible things that you can experience is to lose the spirit of the Lord." This excommunicant sat there and said to himself, "How does he know, unless he has sinned like I have? How does a general authority know?" Well, he reasoned it out in his mind, maybe vicariously one in his position can know, and maybe he has had experience with those who have lost the spirit, so that he knows. With these things on his mind, he went home and began to write, and he put in my hands the results of his thinking. This article is one of the saddest things that I have read in a long time. This man had been a teacher. He said:

"While I was enjoying the spirit of the Holy Ghost, I could read the scriptures and the unfoldment of the truths would come before me, and I was thrilled. That power is gone today. That day . . . I heard that terrible word in the high council trial, 'You are hereby excommunicated,' it was as though a pall of darkness fell, and now instead of light, there is doubt and wavering in my faith. I am wondering and I am struggling without that light. In prayer I used to be able to kneel down and get a tremendous lift from my prayer. Even while I was sinning, even up to the point of my excommunication I got some comfort from it, but now it is as though a dome of steel is over my head, and I seem not to be able to pray. The spirit that leads to the presence of our Father has been lost.

"I used to enjoy performing the ordinances of the Church, especially in behalf of my own children, to bless them, to baptize them, to confirm them, to ordain them to the priesthood; and now to have to stand by while some other takes my place, has been one of the saddest experiences that has come to me. And going to the temple, of course, I have been refused that privilege today. I no longer can go there and enjoy that sweet peace. I stand as though I had never been within those sacred walls. I go to sacrament meeting, I can't partake of the sacrament. I can't even pay my tithing which I realize was a great blessing to me. I have lost the respect of my family. My children tolerate me, but I know that deep in their hearts there is a shame because they bear the name of a father who hasn't lived worthily.

"But the most serious of all my reflections has come when I have contemplated death. Years ago I used to think of death as a contemplation into a great life . . . into the presence of the Lord. Now when I think about it, I have a feeling of horror, and for the first time, I know what the scripture means when it says,

> To those who had died righteously their death shall be sweet unto them, but to those who have died in their evil sinning, bitter shall be their death. The righteous shall not partake of death, though the wicked will die many times. (*Doctrine and Covenants* 42:46-47.)

"I had heard the warnings of these and other unpleasant conditions that would result when the spirit of the Lord was withdrawn because of transgression. The warnings have been given many times by the General Authorities as they come to our meetings to counsel us. How often I failed to heed their warning! How often I have asked myself, probably unconsciously, if they really knew what they were talking about! Now I am being taught the correctness of their words by the most costly of all teachers, experience. I know now that their warnings were inspired. I know now that the conditions they said would follow in the darkness that comes with the loss of the spirit to transgression were as sure to follow as the night follows the day. I add my warning, as one who is being taught by sorrowful, costly experience, to that of the leaders, and give testimony that they know whereof they speak. It is given in hope that some-one will be moved to heed the counsel of these wise men before he too has regrets that cannot be overcome and sorrows that cannot be assuaged." [*Harold B. Lee* 6]

Testimony of a Tough Guy. It was my privilege to become acquainted with the toughest man ever to go inside prison walls—the toughest man I have ever seen. I want to explain what I mean by a tough guy by asking you a question or two. Which is the toughest guy—one who can spit tobacco juice out of his mouth, or the one who can clean it up? Which is the toughest guy—one who can go out Saturday night and say: "I ain't tied to Maw's apron strings. I don't have to go to Church. I can smoke if I want to, I can drink if I want to," or the young fellow who can get up Sunday morning, go to his priesthood meeting and his Sunday School, even when some of his schoolboy companions call him a sissy for going to church? Who is the tough guy? Well, Bill Smith is a tough guy.

As I would come into prison at three o'clock in the afternoon, Bill with about twenty or thirty other inmates in the penitentiary would leave the recreation field and come in and study the Book of Mormon four days a week. They would come to Church Sunday morning. There are gangs in prison as there are gangs outside. There are those in prison who blame the Mormons for everything. They hate the Church. I don't know a single case where a man was put in prison for going to church. And a man who goes to church in prison is a sissy in the eyes of many of his inmates.

Seven of the inmates got together one afternoon. "We're going to teach Bill a lesson." Six of them settled at the foot of the stairs; the seventh man, about a 240 pounder, stood up on the landing. Bill had to come up those steel stairs to go to the second floor to his cell. He passed the six, then came to the seventh man up on the landing. The big fellow bumped him with his shoulder and said, "Out of m' way, sissy!"

Well, Bill's a peaceful fellow; he wouldn't pick a fight with anyone, but he would welcome one if it came walking down the street, and he wouldn't move half an inch. So he reached over and grabbed the big boy by the shoulder and said, "Listen, buddy, you can't do that to me."

The big fellow said, "No? What are you going to do about it?"

Bill said, "Only this," and slapped him aside the face.

They knew that was what would happen. They knew if they would provoke Bill, Bill would hit him. He hit him hard, and he hit him first. That's what they wanted. Now they could report to the officers: "Bill started a brawl." That would put Bill in solitary confinement with bread and water for thirty days. But in the meantime, there they were, seven to one. Now they would tear him apart—make him wish he had never heard of church or Mormons. So there on the landing that big boy squared off and hit my boy Bill. Well, Bill weighs 195 pounds—fighter by trade and by instinct; that's one of the reasons that he was in prison. With all of the 195 pounds that he had he let him have it. Just as you would hit a beef in the slaughter house, the 240 pounds joined his companions at the foot of the stairs. Then he looked at the seven of them down there and said, "Any of you other guys want to take on this sissy?" They had enough sissy for one day. They didn't report to the officers; they took the fallen hero back to his cell.

You know Bill was one of the best missionaries I had inside the walls. I hated to see him get out. I could use Bill in prison. One day he said to me, "Ray, do you know what's wrong with that class you teach?"

I said, "What's wrong with it, Bill?"

He said, "You've got too many darn Mormons in it."

I said, "What do you mean, Bill?"

"You've got a bunch of hypocrites in there, men who brag about being Mormons, and they are the lowest scum we've got inside the walls."

He was talking about three men, three who were once high priests in the Church of Jesus Christ of Latter-day Saints, three men who were sex criminals, three men who were doing everything contrary to the teachings of the Church. I said, "Bill, they are not members of the Church. They were once; they have been excommunicated for what they have done because they are still unrepentant."

He said, "You might know it, but the men out there don't know it. And when I ask them to come to class, when I ask them to come and study with us, they say 'If that's the stuff Ray Smith is teaching, if that's the Mormons, I don't want anything to do with them.' "

I thought, "Is that the way the Church is judged?"

Brothers and sisters, how else can the Church be judged except by the lives of those who profess to belong to it? I am going to say to you this morning, every one of you: someone is looking at you every day of your life, and they are judging the Church by you. Now all of you ask yourself this question: "What kind of a church do I have?"

I was giving a talk to Summit County a few years ago —Aaronic Priesthood Award Night in the South Summit Stake—and I took Bill with me. There in the Kamas Tabernacle I said, "Brothers and sisters, I have that tough guy with me tonight. Bill, will you come up and talk to the boys?"

Bill had never spoken in public; he was only a few months out of prison. He came up to the front and saw that sea of faces going clear back to the amusement hall. He said, "Well, I don't know what to say to you guys, but I can tell you it takes more guts to stand up here and talk than it does to stick a gat in a guy's ribs." I wondered what else he was going to say. Then he gave them a talk I couldn't equal in hours. He said, "Fellows, it isn't worth it. You know I have had a chance to sit in a little four-by-eight and think and think and think. Oh, I have made more money in nine months since I have been out of prison than I made in five years robbing people. I can go down the street now and the car that drives up to the curb isn't a police car after Bill Smith; it's just someone trying to find a parking place. I can be home; the telephone rings—I don't have to run out and hide." He said, "It isn't worth it. There is no glamor in crime, in spite of what you have heard or seen or read."

It took me about thirty minutes to get that big fellow out of the Kamas Tabernacle that evening because of those young boys and their mothers and fathers talking to him.

I am not trying to glamorize a criminal. Bill is not a criminal. He was. I have heard him say, "Thank God, I was sent to prison where I found myself." He said, "I could have killed a man. It wouldn't have mattered to me. I'm a trained fighter. If I saw a man with a wallet or any valuables that I wanted, I walked back of him through a dark alley. I knew right where to hit him, and he never knew what happened. I didn't care whether he ever got up again. That's how low I was. Thank God I was sent to prison." [*Ray F. Smith*]

Missionary Work

Each of Us a Missionary. . . . whether officially commissioned by the Church or not, all of us have the call to be missionaries, to share with our fellowmen the good news that we have heard, the greatness of God and the goodness of his law.

Our mission field may be a nation—or a neighborhood. That does not matter. To one it may be given to tell that story, ever ancient, ever new, through a medium that will reach hundreds of millions of people for generations. Another's life-work may be accomplished when he plants the seed of truth in the soul of a single child. That does not matter either—for who can say which achievement is the greater? What matters, and matters supremely, is not how many things we do, but what we are. [*Cecil B. DeMille*]

Divisions of Missionary Work. . . . there are three subdivisions to missionary work. There are many of you young men and women here who have performed wonderful missions in the world. Now that is one form of a mission, to preach the gospel to the unbelievers in the world. The second form of missionary labor, and I am not trying to classify them as to their importance for they are all equally important, the second great group is the one I first mentioned, the active participants in the Church organizations. They act as missionaries to the membership of the Church and teach them the gospel of Jesus Christ. The third great subdivision is to do the work for the dead, vicariously. [*Henry D. Moyle* 3]

". . . Save It Be One Soul . . ."   I remember the story that
Brother Charles A. Callis used to tell us. There was a missionary who went over to Ireland and filled a mission of
two or three years. They invited him to the stand to give
his homecoming speech and he said something like this,
"Brothers and sisters, I think my mission has been a failure.
I have labored all my days as a missionary here and I have
only baptized one dirty little Irish kid. That is all I baptized."

Years later this man came back, went up to his home
somewhere in Montana, and Brother Callis, now a member
of the Council of the Twelve learned where he was living,
this old missionary, and he went up to visit him. And he
said to him, "Do you remember having served as a missionary over in Ireland? And do you remember having said that
you thought your mission was a failure because you had
only baptized one dirty little Irish kid?"

He said, "Yes."

Well, Brother Callis put out his hand and said, "I
would like to shake hands with you. My name is Charles
A. Callis, of the Council of the Twelve of the Church of
Jesus Christ of Latter-day Saints. I am that dirty little Irish
kid that you baptized on your mission." [*Harold B. Lee* 4]

Industry in Missionary Work. Quite a number of years ago
when I was visiting one of the missions, the mission president asked a young missionary to drive me to my next
appointment. On the way I had the opportunity of talking
to this young man, and he told me something of his missionary efforts. He was very modest about it, but I drew
from him the fact that in his mission, which was just then
closing, he had the good fortune to baptize thirty-four people
into the Church. Naturally I thought that was a splendid
record, and I asked him something of the means employed
to accomplish that result. "Well," he said, "I tried to follow
two or three rules. In the first place, I tried to put in the time.
I think I was never in bed after six o'clock in the morning,
and I seldom got to bed before midnight. In the next place,"

he said, "when I went to visit people I told them I had no time to talk about anything except the gospel, and if they tried to get me to talk about politics, or about the weather or current affairs, I told them I was there to deliver a message to them." . . . Now, of course, that young man had a fine missionary spirit; he had lots of industry and courage and devotion. I met him some years later. I saw that he was in a bishopric and I said, "I guess you don't have much time for missionary work now."

"Oh yes," he said, "I get a little time for missionary work."

"How many have you baptized since you came home?"

"Six."

He then had forty baptisms to his credit. I don't know how many since. He was a man with the missionary spirit and the industry to organize his effort so that it might count in that great work. [*Stephen L Richards* 1]

Baptism in Missionary Work. I remember one time I was down in the central part of Brazil, in a place called Campinas. I was asked to go to the Rotary Club in that city. I discovered, however, that all the proceedings were in Portuguese. I didn't understand too much about what went forward, but I had a Canadian who sat next to me and he interpreted at least some of the major things for me. A Brazilian spoke at the club, in Portuguese. I couldn't understand what he said, but I found that he had the attention of the entire club, and he received an ovation when he finished. I asked my friend who he was, and he said he was a Portuguese businessman who was leaving Campinas for another location, and since this was his last day at the club he gave his final speech.

My Canadian friend told me, "He says he wants to meet you." I couldn't understand why he wanted to meet me, but after the meeting adjourned some friends brought him to me. He couldn't speak English, and I couldn't speak Portuguese; so we were interpreted to each other, and I learned why he wanted to meet me. He said through the interpreter to me, "This day, my daughter is to be baptized into your church." He said, "I am greatly agitated and worried about it. I have given my consent, but she is the first one in all the generations of our family of which we have knowledge who has ever left the church of her forefathers." He added, "I must now go to my home and try to comfort my family."

He was very upset, and I said, "My friend don't worry; your daughter will be happy and she will make you all happy." That's about all I could say to him through the interpreter. He went away and later that afternoon I went to the baptismal service. It was about fifteen miles distant on a turbulent river. I was fearful for the safety of those who went into that river—it was so swift. But they found an eddy near the bank, and the baptismal service proceeded. About eight candidates for baptism appeared. I was very thrilled with the one who officiated at the service. Above the roar of the river you could hear his clear voice as he raised his hand and repeated those solemn words. "Having been commissioned of Jesus Christ, I baptize you in the name of the Father, and of the Son, and of the Holy Ghost." Everyone was thrilled. After the service I was sitting in a car, because it was raining, when this man who had approached me earlier in the day came to the open window of the car, extended his hand through the window to me, and said, for the first time speaking in English, "I have peace." I'm sure that the influence of that great service, baptizing his daughter into the Kingdom of God, had brought with it a spirit which had comforted his agitated and worried heart.

I know of nothing greater than baptism to bring happiness and peace and joy. And so those who would go forth to bless mankind can find no more worthy endeavor than to try to bring about the baptism of our Father's children into his Church and kingdom. [*Stephen L Richards* 1]

Morals

Challenge to Be Morally Clean. I called on the president of the stake to speak at the morning session of conference. There was in the old tabernacle a balcony in the back end of the room that I suppose held about two hundred people. I observed that that balcony was filled entirely with young folk, the lower floor was packed with older folk and children. When I called on the president of the stake to speak, he got up, and he looked directly at the young folk in that balcony. He said this to them in substance: "Young people, nearly every one of you will be coming to me as your stake president pretty soon for a recommend, some to go on missions, some to be married, some for promotion in the priesthood. When each one of you comes, I will sit him or her down in the chair right in front of me, and I will look him or her squarely in the eye, and I will ask one question, 'Are you clean?' If you can answer yes, you will be happy. If you answer no, you will be sorry. If you lie to me, you will regret it all the days of your life." That is all he said and sat down. There was a profound silence. I am sure that the challenge of that president of the stake will never be forgotten by his young folk. [*Stephen L Richards* 4]

Personal Responsibility for Moral Living. When it comes to the matter of your moral life, are you stable or are you unstable? And remember that you are not to suppose that you are by nature unstable and that therefore you can not do anything about it. We have young people who come and tell us about their sins, and they say that because they believe they are made as they are, they can not do anything about it. God made them that way they claim, saying they are victims of circumstances, and so they don't try to overcome their weakness. That is a false philosophy. [*Mark E. Petersen* 3]

Carnal versus Righteous Experience. Carnal experience as such, regardless of how aesthetically, emotionally or physically compelling or tremendous it may be, has been and always will be an end in itself—an end that when carried to its extreme is called death—and after the climatic moments of fulfillment are accomplished, leaves the soul unsatisfied, debased and with an inevitable haunting sense of self-betrayal. Righteous experience has been and always will be, not an end in itself, but a personal expression of eternal life, soul-satisfying, exalting and productive of the Godly attributes of eternal beauty, purity, truth, yes, even life-creation itself. Carnal passion produces an ecstacy to destruction and damnation. Righteous passion produces an ecstacy to life and exaltation.

It is for a member of the Church of Jesus Christ of Latter-day Saints then, not only the privilege, but the duty, to discern in himself righteous passion from carnal passion through the exercise of the gift of the Holy Ghost, enabling him, at least to a limited degree, to see these things as God sees them, comprehend the issues as God comprehends them. [*Lynn A. McKinlay*]

Obedience

Love versus Discipline. . . . if the Lord loves us and desires that we have joy, why does he give so many commandments, many of them restrictive in their nature? Well, the obvious answer is because he loves us, and he wishes us to be saved from sorrow and remorse and from losing our blessings.

While I was attending a conference in California some time ago, I was told about one of our members whose business it is to assist others in trouble; he was given permission to interview a young man who had been in serious difficulties with the law and was serving a sentence in prison. The interviewer asked this young man this question: "Would you mind giving me the dominant reason for your being here in this situation?"

After a moment of thought, this young man replied, "I am here because no one loved me enough to correct me." [*ElRay L. Christiansen 2*]

Love versus Fear. Sometimes I am afraid that some people, even some of our parents, are trying to frighten us into the celestial glory. There is no place in the plan, which is to give us peace, for frightening God's children back into his presence. I think the sweetest words ever uttered were these three, "God is love." And where love is obtained in the world or in the home or in the hearts of man, there will be and abide peace.

If you are obedient, lift up your hearts and rejoice. Be joyous, be happy. There is no purpose in all of this obedience if there is no provision in that obedience for a peace of mind and a tranquility of soul. Have peace in your hearts; have peace of mind; and then let that influence, or effluence, or whatever you would call it, carry over into the lives of others. Don't try to frighten people with the plan of peace. You know as well as I that what this world lacks today, is the influence of the Prince of Peace. [*Matthew Cowley* 3]

Pioneer Virtues. Many noble, yet confused young people, and old ones for that matter, are starving for a few forthright answers to their questions. They yearn for dependable direction, but instead of bread we often give them a stone. Instead of direction we often add to their confusion. Why don't we refer them to those pioneer virtues that have made America a great country? Why don't we tell them that the Church speaks with authority in an age of confusion, not dogmatically but in terms of good will, that they will be far safer and happier if they stay with the Ten Commandments, the Sermon on the Mount, and the greatest commandment of Jesus, at least until the world finds something better, and I certify that we have found nothing better. [*Henry Aldous Dixon*]

Obedience to Law. The gospel of Jesus Christ teaches that to be happy and to enjoy life fully, we must live in obedience to law—the physical law, the intellectual law, and the spiritual law—and that unhappiness results when one disregards the laws of life. . . . [*ElRay L. Christiansen*]

God No Respecter of Persons. Sometimes young people get the idea—and it is erroneous—they are just a little different from the other fellow, that the rules that apply to the masses do not apply to them. Be assured, . . . that the author of this universe, the God of this world, our Father, is not capricious, he has no favorites—his laws are universal, eternal, inexorable; and anyone who violates the law must pay the penalty. I prefer the positive approach, however: All who obey the law will get the blessing. [*Hugh B. Brown* 2]

Keeping God's Commandments. We are happier, our conscience is clearer, and our lives are more acceptable to God and man if we show our love for and dependence on God by living and keeping his commandments. Nothing will give us that feeling of security and peace of mind as the knowledge that God lives and that we are keeping in tune with his spirit and living in harmony with his teachings. . . . [*Neldon E. Tanner*]

Obedience and Happiness. I'm sure that I need not reaffirm my conviction here that the way to happiness is to learn and obey and share the principles of the gospel of Jesus Christ. No scriptural teaching known to me is more patently true than that ignorance and wickedness and selfishness do not bring happiness. [*Marion D. Hanks* 3]

They who observe the law will find freedom within the law. Obedience to law is liberty. [*Hugh B. Brown* 2]

Obedience and Adversity. God does not promise us then, escape from affliction or adversity as a reward for obedience. He does not guarantee us immunity from germs or disease or difficulty, from war, or from the effects of the laws of gravity or of force and motion. We gratefully accepted the ineffably important opportunity to come to a world where these problems were to be present, and would be, until men, with proper use of their eternal agency, learned to conquer them, or until he came to live again among men. [*Marion D. Hanks* 3]

Intelligent Obedience. It's possible to keep the law of obedience perfectly—to learn how to listen to counsel, not blindly but intelligently. I had a man who taught me that lesson a few years ago. He was a candidate in a political party, and there came out a rather strong statement from the editorial page of the *Deseret News*—put on the front page where everybody could see it. It was a serious blow to the party of which he was a member, and when I met him on the street a little while later I said, "Did you read the editorial?" (I knew he couldn't have missed it.)

He said, "Yes, I read it and immediately I said to myself, 'Well, I know what the brethren are counseling. I shall do what they have counseled.' But," he added to me, "I didn't feel right in my heart about it. I was quarreling within myself. It took a whole night on my knees praying before I could feel right in accepting the counsel that has thus been given."

President Brigham Young said, "The greatest fear I have is that the members of the Church will accept what we say without praying about it and then getting the witness in their heart that what we say is the will of the Lord." That puts upon every individual the responsibility of getting the witness in order that he can intelligently obey the counsel that comes from the authorities of the Church. [*Harold B. Lee* 2]

Patriarchal Blessings

Mission of a Patriarch. The mission of a patriarch is to reveal the calling of the Lord unto his children here upon the earth so that they will have some concept of what the Lord expects of them while they are here in mortality. [*LeGrand Richards* 1]

Purpose of Patriarchal Blessings. One of the purposes of patriarchal blessings is to give unto us the inspiration that will enable us to make good here in mortality, that we will be worthy of the great calling that came to us before the foundation of the world. [*LeGrand Richards* 1]

Inspiration in Patriarchal Blessings. A couple of boys came to the patriarch to receive their blessings. The patriarch knew one of the boys very well, and to that one he said, "I have a wonderful blessing for you." He blessed the other boy first. And when he laid his hands on the head of the other boy (the one he said he had a wonderful blessing for) he could not give him a blessing at all. The words just would not come. Finally he had to say, "You will have to come back some other time." The Lord let that patriarch know that no patriarch has a blessing for anybody. The blessings are from the Lord. [*LeGrand Richards* 1]

Pioneers

In the memoirs of John R. Young, a Utah pioneer of 1847, is an interesting account of an incident that occurred on the trail from Nauvoo to Winter Quarters in the early spring of 1846. It involved a young convert, Orson Spencer, who, a few years previously, had joined the Latter-day Saints Church in Massachusetts and later in Utah was appointed the first president of the University of Deseret.

Orson Spencer was reared in the same state that gave to America such illustrious personalities as John Adams, Henry W. Longfellow, and Louisa May Alcott. He, himself, was a graduate of two colleges and was trained for the ministry.

While still in his young manhood, he courted and became engaged to marry a very lovely young lady, daughter of one of the wealthiest families of the community. It was at this time that two Mormon missionaries arrived in this community. They began preaching the restored gospel as taught by the Prophet Joseph Smith and the Latter-day Saints. Orson Spencer heard their message, was converted and baptized.

When the parents of the young lady, to whom he was engaged, learned of his conversion, they advised their daughter that should she marry Orson Spencer they would disown her, disinherit her and never permit her to return to their home. Disregarding this threat, she married Orson Spencer, continued to live in the same community, and had five children.

In about 1840, they moved to Nauvoo, Illinois, where the Mormon people were gathering and during the next five years passed through the terrible persecutions of that period. Sister Spencer was unaccustomed to the life she was forced to live during those painful years in Nauvoo and gradually lost her health.

Then, one day, President Brigham Young announced that arrangements were being made for the people to journey west. Due to her ill health, it was necessary that she be carried on an improvised cot to the covered wagon in which the Spencer family were to travel.

They crossed the Mississippi River on ice and followed the frozen trail westward through Iowa. The traveling was terrible. During the day the sun would shine, melt the ice and the road would become a sea of mud, only to be frozen over again during the night. So bad were conditions that Orson Spencer wrote his wife's parents asking permission to bring his wife back to their home until she recovered her health.

One evening, after being on the trail eighteen days, he was out caring for his cattle when Porter Rockwell rode into camp with the mail from Nauvoo. The mail was a letter from his wife's parents addressed to Orson Spencer in which they reaffirmed their former position. Yes, they would deeply appreciate having their daughter back; they would be thrilled—but not as a member of the Mormon Church.

Orson Spencer took the letter to the covered wagon where his wife lay desperately ill. Then by the light of the lantern, he read to her her parents' letter. Then upon bended knees, with tears trickling down his cheeks, he pleaded with her to permit him to take her back to Nauvoo.

To his pleading she looked up with a faint smile and said, "Orson, the Bible is in a box there in the corner of the wagon. Will you hand it to me?" In compliance with her request, he brought the Bible to her and she then said,

"Now turn to the first chapter of the Book of Ruth and read aloud the fifteenth and sixteenth verses.

He read the following:

"Entreat me not to leave thee—or to return from following after thee; for whither thou goest, I will go:—And thy people shall be my people, and thy God my God." (Ruth 1:16.)

He ceased reading. He returned the Bible to its place and then in turning to his wife, he was startled to see a peculiar pallor creeping across her countenance; he saw her eyelids drop and then they were closed, he knew never to open again in mortality.

On the following morning, there by the side of the road on that lonely Iowa prairie, in a shallow grave, they laid to rest this wonderful woman, to the music only of the lowing of the cattle.

Within an hour, the caravan was again on its way, and Orson Spencer sat alone with his five little kiddies driving westward, westward to his destiny. The eldest of those little kiddies took the place of the mother, and when that little girl grew to womanhood she became the founder of the Primary Association of the Church. [*Nicholas G. Morgan, Sr.*]

Practical Religion

Sister Longden and I had another experience a few years ago while I was associated with one of the large companies of the United States. The president of that organization and his wife visited in Salt Lake City for the first time. His wife had been a school teacher and she was much impressed with the culture of the Latter-day Saints. They had several married children. We showed them the points of interest in Salt Lake City—the tabernacle, the Lion House and Welfare Square. I was grateful that evening to entertain them at dinner in our own home.

We had a rich experience as we sat around the table, long after the meal had been consumed. Our children were there with us. We talked about many things, and finally this gentleman said, "You know, I have been very much interested today, especially in the tour that you have given us and the final visit to Welfare Square. I've read something about your Church; I know something of your history; I've read about Joseph Smith and Brigham Young. I know how Joseph Smith started this Church. I've read that there was much persecution, that there were many revivals at that time in numerous churches." He said, "Many of those churches have disintegrated and are not in existence today, but your Church has continued through the years. Today I have learned the reason why."

And I said, "What is the reason?"

He replied, "Because you have a practical religion, a practical religion that can apply every day and every hour, and every minute of your lives. I've seen that religion in action today." [*John Longden*]

Prayer

Prayer and the Restoration of the Gospel. He [Joseph Smith] was a prayerful man. It was a prayer that brought forth the first vision. It was a prayer that brought the Angel Moroni, who revealed to him the hiding place of the sacred record, to his bedside. It was a prayer that brought John the Baptist, who conferred upon Joseph and Oliver the Aaronic Priesthood and taught them the proper method of baptism. Prayer preceded almost every revelation recorded in the Doctrine and Covenants. Prayer was one of the foundation stones of Joseph's great and successful career. [*Preston Nibley*]

Prayer a Source of Strength. If we would advance in holiness—increase in favor with God—nothing can take the place of prayer. And so I adjure you . . . to give prayer—daily prayer—secret prayer—a foremost place in your lives. Let no day pass without it. Whatever else you must give up, do not forego prayer.

Communion with the Almighty has been a source of strength, inspiration and enlightenment to men and women —through the world's history—who have shaped the destinies of individuals and nations for good. In your own lives many of you have doubtless come to the profound realization that man does not stand alone. With all our learning and capacity for future growth, we recognize many serious limitations. It is the part of wisdom to acknowledge and experience that there is an unseen source of power and truth. There are "hidden treasures." He who is able to avail himself of this blessing in life is free as the boundless universe. He who does not, dwarfs his own potential. He effectively shuts the door on the greatest source of knowledge, power and joy that is available to man.

Will you value and take advantage of the opportunity to tap these unseen but very real spiritual powers? Will you with Lincoln before Gettysburg and Washington at Valley Forge humble yourselves before Almighty God in fervent prayers? Will you be able to affirm the solemn declaration of one of America's eminent scientist-educators, Dr. John A. Widtsoe, a man who in his lifetime was president of two of America's fine educational institutions as he said:

Men who search out truth are prayerful. They stand with uncovered heads before the unknown. They know their own insignificance before the eternal fount of knowledge . . . Manly men who really love truth, are proud to pray to God for help and guidance. They get down on their knees . . . To win knowledge of the unseen, to obtain a testimony of truth, one must pray without ceasing. It must be the first and the last act of the day.

Prayer will help you understand the apparent conflicts in life—to know that God lives, that life is eternal.

Again, I adjure you to value this practice and seek throughout your lives the blessings of daily secret prayer.

Prayer will increase your faith in God—and your trust and love—so that whatever trials and difficulties life may hold for you, you may say with Job: "I know that my redeemer liveth." [*Ezra Taft Benson* 3]

Prayers Will Be Answered. Some of you folks never have had the experience of having something happen to you which assures you that prayer can be answered. I can assure everyone of you, that if you believe in the Eternal Father, that he is a being of person, that he is your Father, that you are his sons and daughters, that Jesus Christ is the Redeemer of the world, that he is also a person, and that you may become like him—if those things you believe, then you may be sure that there will come a time in your life, if you keep at it, when there will be no doubt in your souls that your prayers will be answered for your good. [*S. Dilworth Young*]

How Should We Pray?   Some time ago I was in the New England Mission. Incidental to my being there, I became acquainted with a very splendid Christian minister. I think the gentleman could give us odds on how to behave from the standpoint of being Christian. I've never known a man who spends so much time loving humanity as he does, and actually in doing things for them to prove it. He has in his home a place where he retires every morning for meditation and prayer. In there is a cross hanging on the wall, and as I recall it, a place for a couple of candles, though I wouldn't be certain of that now. And there in this room, facing this symbol of our Lord, he, I suppose, first thinks a while, then reads, perhaps to himself aloud. After this he probably opens his Bible, and eventually I think he must get on his knees and pray.

He came to call upon us many times while we were there and stayed with us several times overnight; consequently, he became a part of our own devotions. We were quite abrupt about it. Can you see us in our mission home now? I know the missionaries can. It's time for breakfast, and so we shall have prayer first. Now some mission homes don't do it this way, but we did, so I'll have to tell it the way we did it. We would all rush into the library. A check was made to see if all were present. If anyone was missing, we would wait a moment and if they didn't come, we'd commence without them. At a signal from me, which was usually a nod of the head, we'd all kneel down quickly right where we were, and then whoever was called upon would offer a prayer—no preliminaries, no building up of the spirit —just plain, ordinary prayer.

Then we'd arise and rush in to the breakfast table, sit down, and someone would mumble, like we always do, one of those standard church blessings on the food. And because we knew them off by heart so well, they'd usually be very rapidly said. I've often wondered, what that man thought about us as spiritual people. What did he think of his way of reaching into the infinite toward Deity as compared with our close association with our Father on such a plane that it would sound as though we were going to slap him on the back the next minute? [*S. Dilworth Young*]

An Answer to a Humble Prayer.   I heard from a president and his wife returning from a mission over in East Germany behind the Iron Curtain about a young girl attending school there. In the discussions of her class the teacher had learned that she was a Latter-day Saint and believed in God. He scoffed at the idea of a God and to punish her he said, "You must write fifty times, 'There is no God.' "

She took that terrible assignment to her mother and her mother said, "You mustn't write, 'There is no God,' my dear. There is a God."

She went back and when he found that she had not written what he had commanded he said, "Go back again and write one hundred times, that 'There is no God' and if you don't write it by tomorrow there will be something terrible happen."

The next day she came, after she and her mother had spent nearly all night on their knees praying to that God about whom the teacher had commanded she should write, "There is no God," but she said, "I can't." And her mother said, "No, you must not write, 'There is no God.' "

The next morning the mother went with her daughter to school. They went out and stood by the door waiting for the teacher to come. The principal of the school came walking by and said, "Were you waiting for Mr. so and so," naming the teacher of that room.

They said, "Yes."

"Well," the principal said, "I am sorry to inform you that this morning we just received word that he died suddenly of a heart attack. He won't be here today." Something terrible did happen but it wasn't to the girl of faith. Better that one lose his life than to deny the testimony of the divinity of the Savior of this world. [*Harold B. Lee* 4]

Praying in Prison. A man came into class one day. [In the Utah State Prison] He said, "Well, I'll come 'n an' study with you, but no prayin'. I ain't goin' to pray."

I said, "All right, Dick, there will be no praying." We opened and closed our study group with prayer, of course.

After about three months of four days a week, one afternoon the man in charge of the study group said, "Dick, will you give our closing prayer?" And Dick did. After that he took his turn with the other thirty-five or forty men, opening and closing our study group with prayer.

Then came a Sunday morning I want to tell you about. Sunday morning is different from study groups. Sunday morning they [the prisoners] have their free agency as you have it here. They either come to church or stay locked up in their cells. Most of them come to church. One Sunday morning as I came into church, the secretary handed me a piece of paper with two names on it; Dick was to give the opening prayer. I announced the opening song and said, "Dick Brown will give the opening prayer." Dick came up, stood at the side of the old platform, said a few words in prayer, and went back to his seat. I went on with the meeting.

The next day after class he said, "Ray, I want to talk to you a minute."

I said, "What's on your mind, Dick?"

He said, "I want to talk to you about that prayer yesterday."

I put my arm around him and said, "All right, that's fine, Dick. I was proud of you to hear you pray before that group of men."

He said, "That isn't what I mean. I don't care what I said. I want to talk to you about that prayer. I knew I was going to have to pray; they had asked me previously. But when I came into church that morning, I could feel a spirit of evil there, just as if the very devil himself was there. Then you announced the opening song and said I was to give the opening prayer. I didn't have to be by those men; I knew what they were all saying and all whispering to one another, 'Dick, Dick Brown's going to pray! That old hypocrite's hanging on to Smith, trying to get out of jail!' I knew what they were all saying. All during that opening song I had that terrible feeling. It seemed I had to walk about two miles from where I sat to the front. I turned around and I said, 'Our Father in Heaven . . .' A feeling came over me such as I have never experienced in all my life. It was as though I stood in the air. I knew the gospel of Jesus Christ was true, and I didn't care what anyone thought; I knew what I was doing was right."

That morning, unknown to any of us, in the Utah State Prison, the Lord performed a miracle; he gave a boy a testimony of the gospel—the boy who wouldn't pray.

Dick was going to be released in six months; three months later, however, he went over the fence in an escape attempt. I could tell you why but I am not going into that. He was arrested within a few hours and was put in solitary confinement. When he came back to class he said, "Ray, they are going to try me for escape. I wish you would come down and be a character witness for me."

I went down to court and answered a few questions for the lawyer. Then they argued the case before the jury. The jury went into the jury room for a decision; the judge retired to his chambers. Dick was handcuffed again to the clerk of the penitentiary. The guard took him over toward the door. On the way over he said, "Mr. Dent, can I talk to Ray for a minute?"

Mr. Dent said, "You surely can," and he unlocked the handcuffs.

Dick said, "Ray, I want you to pray with me." Dick didn't want me to pray; Dick wanted to pray.

There in Judge Baker's courtroom, on the third floor of the City and County Building in Salt Lake City, Dick and I knelt by the table, and there I heard the most humble prayer I have ever heard in my church experience. I heard a boy talk to his Heavenly Father as if his Heavenly Father was on the other side of the table.

I am not so sure that He wasn't. Did he pray that he might be found innocent? He said, "Our Father in Heaven, regardless of the verdict, may I never become bitter in my heart. May the testimony you gave me of the truthfulness of the gospel of Jesus Christ never leave me."

His prayer was answered. He was found guilty; that's the state law, and he was sentenced to one to ten more years in prison. He served two and a half years of that time. I have heard him get up in sacrament meeting and say, "Thank God I was sent to prison where I received a testimony of the gospel." Dick died with that testimony. He also died a violent death. Some of you remember two years ago a man who died of exposure on a deer hunt. That was my friend Dick, the boy who wouldn't pray. [*Ray F. Smith*]

Pray Always. We should pray always, according to divine direction. We should pray over our flocks, our herds, our children, our homes, our books, our examinations, our ball games; over our problems, our joys, our gratitudes, our great experiences. We should be prayerful in attitude and in fact. I believe I have learned how to pray. The prayers that I have learned to offer are not literarily noteworthy, nor greatly involved, nor very long. I'll give you an example.

A man came to Temple Square one day and stood outside the office door, wanting to come in. I knew as I saw him that he had a desperate need, and I'll confess, to my sorrow, that my first thought was that the need probably was economic. We have many occasions there to be blessed with such opportunities. Well, I looked at him just a little bit suspiciously, and then going to the door, I invited him in and saw immediately in his face that the need he had

had little to do with economics. He had a kind of glaze over his eyes that comes with a deep shattering shock.

He was a a non-member of the Church, married to a fine Primary president. This lady and he were the parents of a beautiful daughter, age eleven. This man's parents lived in the eastern part of the country, and the family had decided in a little council (a sweet and fine thing as he discussed it) that the best Christmas present they could give his parents was to send Daddy to see them, because it had been so long, and it being Christmas time, the best gift they could receive was a visit from their only son. So he had, although reluctantly, accepted this commission and had gone to see his parents. While there he had received word from people at home that his wife had been in an automobile accident. The little girl had been killed. Through fire that followed, her body had been destroyed.

This was, of course, a terrible shock to him. He was on his way home, and had several hours layover in Salt Lake, and had come to the Temple Square trying to find peace. He sat across the desk from me and I tried to teach him. I have seldom been more frustrated, because I didn't get by that shock at all. I talked of eternity; I talked of resurrection; I talked of the faith we need, of the strength and sustaining influence of the Lord, and nothing registered— nothing at all. I began to get desperate. He sat, ill at ease, and getting ready to move, and I began to pray. My prayer, and I have repeated it so many times under similar circumstances, was, "Lord, help me now." "Lord, help me now." And for a reason I am sure of, and you will accept I suppose, I opened this book—perhaps I should have done it much sooner without the stimulus of the inspiration, but hadn't— to these words out of the eleventh chapter of the Book of Alma:

The spirit and the body shall be reunited again in its perfect form; both limb and joint shall be restored to its proper frame, . . . (Alma 11:43.)

I turned to Alma 40, and read a little more of the resurrection, that ". . . even a hair of our heads would not be lost. . . . " Alma 40:23.) For the first time I saw the break come. I found as we talked that the thing that disturbed him most was that this beautiful little girl—and I have little girls; I know about how a father would feel, at least I think I can imagine—the thing that bothered him most was that he could not even see her again, that the beauty and perfection of her little life was gone, and he had no real hope for anything more. But he sat and listened, and the simple therapy was repeated. We read it as the word of the Lord. He accepted it as such. He sat in one of those little alcoves near the door and read it over and over for a long time. When I took him to the airport, the glaze in his eye was gone. He had wept, perhaps for the first time. He had talked and seemed reachable, and we had discussed the principles I had tried to talk of before.

A few months later I heard his voice at the counter. I hadn't heard a thing from him since our first meeting. He was standing there with two rather rough looking men. They turned out to be his wife's brothers, born in the Church. He had a copy of the Book of Mormon opened to Alma 11 and was reading to them those wonderful words, testifying of their truth, telling them that in his search through the record he had found it to be the word of God. He bought a book for them and sent them home to read, these men who had been born into the faith. . . . We must "pray always" if we would have what we seek. [*Marion D. Hanks* 4]

Pre-Existence

Pre-existence Reasonable. The Lord made the principle of pre-existence very clear in the revelations which have come to us through the Prophet Joseph Smith and others, and it is reasonable doctrine. It answers that one great question which comes into the mind of every normal individual, "From whence did I come?" The doctrine of an eternal spirit inhabiting a mortal body, which spirit continues after the death of the body, is quite generally accepted, but there are comparatively few who believe in the doctrine of a pre-existent life—at least they do not understand it sufficiently. This is indeed strange, because it is a doctrine which is consistent with reason. [*ElRay L. Christiansen* 2]

Purpose of Mortality. We are taught in our scriptures that we are the sons and daughters of God, that he is literally our Father, the Father of our spirits, that we dwelt in his presence, and that we have seen him. . . and when we came into this world all our former knowledge and understanding was taken away and for a wise purpose was erased. But there in that spirit world we had not reached, nor could we reach, the end of our existence, that is, the ultimate reward. It was essential that the opportunity be given to us, to come to this earth where we could receive bodies of flesh and bones, tabernacles for our spirits. [*Joseph Fielding Smith* 1]

Creation an On-going Process. You have been taught that you were intelligences originally, that intelligence was not nor can it be created, that man is spirit, that the elements are eternal and that spirit and element inseparably connected receive a fullness of joy. You have also been taught that creation is an on-going process, and that man has the high privilege of co-operating with God, in the great drama of creation. You have noted already in your studies that the world is not yet fully created or finished, that the Creator left it largely as raw material to set us thinking, experimenting, risking and adventuring. [*Hugh B. Brown* 4]

Mortality and Adversity. We knew before we were born that we were coming to the earth for bodies and experience and that we would have joys and sorrows, pain and comforts, ease and hardships, health and sickness, successes and disappointments, and we knew also that we would die. We accepted all these eventualities with a glad heart, eager to accept both the favorable and unfavorable. We were undoubtedly willing to have a mortal body even if it were deformed. We eagerly accepted the chance to come earthward, even though it might be for a day, a year, or a century. Perhaps we were not so much concerned whether we should die of disease, of accident, or of senility. We were willing to come and take life as it came and as we might organize and control it, and this without murmur, complaint or unreasonable demands. We sometimes think we would like to know what was ahead, but sober thought brings us back to accepting life a day at a time, and magnifying and glorifying that day. [*Spencer W. Kimball* 2]

Priesthood

Priesthood and Keys. What is the priesthood? The priesthood is the power and authority of God delegated to man on earth to act in all things for the salvation of men.

What are the keys? The keys, as used in connection with priesthood and the Church and the kingdom, are the right of presidency; that is, they are the directing power, the ability to designate how and under what circumstances the priesthood will be used, and to regulate and govern all of the affairs of the Church which is the kingdom. [*Bruce R. McConkie* 3]

Fullness of the Gospel. Once the keys were given [to Joseph Smith], once all of the powers and authorities had been restored, we had what is called the fullness of the gospel. The fullness of the gospel does not necessarily consist in having the fullness of knowledge, in knowing all things or having all doctrine revealed or interpreted to us. But the fullness of the gospel in its nature and by definition consists in having all of the keys and all of the power and all of the authority that is necessary to seal men up so that they may inherit a fullness of reward, meaning exaltation in the kingdom hereafter. [*Bruce R. McConkie* 3]

Valid Ordinances. . . . [there are] three great things to which all ordinances must conform. First, the proper thing must be done. If it is baptism, the proper baptism must be performed. Second, it must be done by someone who is a legal administrator, someone who holds the keys and the priesthood and the power, and to whom the Lord has said,

"You may bind on earth and I will recognize it as being sealed in heaven." And third, the ordinance must be sealed by the Holy Spirit of Promise. Now that involves righteousness, personal righteousness, on the part of the participating parties. [*Bruce R. McConkie* 2]

Functions of the Priesthood. ... one of the great functions of the Holy Priesthood of the Lord is to bring to all of the people the concepts and the advice and admonition which may be regarded as essential for the perfection of the Saints, because, after all, there are two major objectives of the Church: first, to perfect the lives of the Saints; and secondly, to proclaim the gospel throughout the world. [*Stephen L Richards* 4]

Powers of Aaronic Priesthood. The powers and prerogatives contained in the Aaronic Priesthood are as follows: first, the keys of the ministering of angels. If you will, contemplate for a moment what it means for men upon the earth to receive the ministering of angels when such ministrations are necessary. In my mind, there is no question but what young men who hold the Aaronic Priesthood, if in their priesthood work are in need of the ministering of angels, they shall enjoy that blessing; but, of course, this is all predicated upon living lives that are compatible with the priesthood that they hold. Contemplate, if you will, the divine right and authority to preach the gospel of repentance, the authority to baptize in the name of the Father and the Son and the Holy Ghost for the remission of sins. When a priest stands in the waters of baptism and raises his arm to the square, pronouncing the name of the candidate to be baptized and repeats the baptismal prayer, it must confirm in his heart that he actually holds the divine right to perform this ordinance, and that it will be recognized in the heavens. [*Joseph L. Wirthlin*]

Senior Aaronic Priesthood In one of our priesthood leadership meetings it was announced that the president of a senior deacons' quorum would address the meeting, and coming out of the audience was a man with snow-white hair. As he took his place on the stand, he said, "Brethren, I am seventy-two years of age. I am so grateful that I have been found worthy to preside over a deacons' quorum in this Church." He continued by explaining some of the experiences he was having—those that impressed him—and he finally said, "I would like to tell you this—that I have just lost seventy-two of the best years of my life. Don't you lose them!" [*Carl W. Buehner*]

Aaronic Priesthood Missionaries. One of the greatest early day missionaries was a priest. President Wilford Woodruff as a young man held the office of an ordained teacher, but there burned in his heart an earnest desire to preach the gospel, and in response to this desire, he supplicated the Lord mightily to the end that he might have the privilege of preaching the gospel. When he arose from his knees, there came in his bosom an assurance that somewhere and sometime he would have the long desired privilege of expounding the gospel. As he walked out of the woods where he had been praying, he met a brother, a high priest, who said, "Brother Woodruff, I think you should be ordained a priest." His prayer was answered at once. With the office of priest resting upon his shoulders, he was called upon a mission into the states of Arkansas and Tennessee, and performed one of the outstanding missionary works of the Church. [*Joseph L. Wirthlin*]

Return to Priesthood Activity. At a quarterly conference in Salt Lake not long ago I remember hearing a man say, "As a deacon, I was a hundred-percenter. When I was ordained a teacher, I was all but perfect—maybe missed twice during the whole period that I was an ordained teacher. When I was ordained a priest in the Aaronic Priesthood, I began to run with some boys who had little interest in the Church, and before I knew it, I was gone. To this day, I wonder where my bishop was; why he didn't miss a young man who had been a hundred-percenter as a deacon and all but a hundred-percenter as a teacher, and who now was not coming to his priesthood meeting at all.

"As I drifted away, I acquired some bad habits, and after three or four years of this kind of living, I met a very charming girl. I decided I would like to have her for my wife, and she finally accepted even though she wanted to marry a young man who could take her to the temple. She had the hope that she could bring me back into activity in the Church. Well, I still went my way; she went hers. Our family began to come; she took the youngsters to Church, and I wandered off where I had been prior to the time I was married.

"One day my oldest boy—now twelve years of age—came home bubbling over with enthusiasm, and he said, 'Dad, what do you think happened to me today? The bishop called me into his office and said, "I have had my eye on you, young man. I have noticed your devotion and faithfulness to your meetings, and I would like to tell you that you are worthy now to hold the Aaronic Priesthood and to be ordained to the office of a deacon in that priesthood." ' "

The father said that his son mentioned a number of other things which the bishop explained to him regarding the value of being a bearer of the priesthood, and then this man said, "You know, I became so enthusiastic that I began to add to what the bishop had stated and said, 'Son, nothing will ever come into your life as important or valuable as holding the priesthood.' While I was speaking to my son, all of a sudden he said to me, 'Well, Dad, if this is such a good thing for me, what is wrong with it for you?' That really pulled me up by the bootstraps, and I decided I would do something about it, but it wasn't easy. I had become steeped in some sins that were difficult to shake off, and it took a long time before I got rid of those bad habits.

"But, finally the day came when I decided I would like to go to priesthood meeting. Three different Sunday mornings I got up and dressed myself, walked over to the meeting-house and up the steps, got my hand on the front doorknob, and then did not have the courage to turn the knob. Three Sunday mornings, I turned around and walked home again. During this period, the only spiritual lift that actually came to me was through the visits of my ward teachers—two wonderful men. They came every month. They didn't spend very much time, but they always left a good message and were very cheerful.

"Two weeks after this last experience of attempting to go to priesthood meeting, my ward teachers came again. The experience was similar to the other visits I had had, except, as they were leaving to go, for some reason or other the senior companion said, 'Say, John, how would you like to have me come next Sunday morning and take you to priesthood meeting?' That struck me like a bolt of lightning, and I all but jumped out of my chair to hug that fellow. I told him to come. He came the next Sunday, and we went to priesthood meeting together. There I met the bishopric and nearly every man who attended priesthood meeting that morning."

This man then made this rather significant statement, "You'll never know how wonderful it is to be on the inside looking out, rather than on the outside trying to get in." [*Carl W. Buehner*]

"Reproving Betimes with Sharpness." I had a remarkable incident come to my attention while on board a ship on the way from South America a number of years ago. I made the acquaintance of a retired minister, advanced in age, who was a very fine gentleman. I was asked to conduct the ship's "divine services," as they were called. We didn't have any-body else of our faith, so I asked this man if he would offer the prayer, and he gave a lovely prayer.

I was telling him a little about our concept of the priest-hood, and when I told him about "reproving with sharp-ness," he said, "I had an interesting experience once. A young man belonging to a family among my parishioners took up the habit of drink, and he simply lost control of himself. He had a wife and two or three little children, and he was the source of great distress and sorrow to his parents, to his wife, and family. One day," said the minister, "I met that young man coming down the street, and when he came to me he proffered his hand to shake hands with me but I didn't shake hands with him. I don't know why," he said, "but I didn't shake hands with him. But I said to him, 'John, I rebuke you, in the name of the Lord Jesus Christ, for your unseemly conduct and the sorrow and disgrace that you are bringing to your family.' "

He said the young man was stunned with that kind of a reception, and the minister said, "I went on, and when I got a little way I said to myself, 'Why in the world did I do that? I have never before been guilty of an offense so ungracious.' " "But," he said, "it wasn't long before that young man came and said to me, 'It seemed as if I couldn't quit my bad habits until that day I met you on the street and you rebuked me as you did. It brought me to a realization of what I was doing. Now I have mustered the courage to stop my bad habits. For a period of weeks now I have overcome them, and I thank you for the rebuke which you gave to me.' "

Then I got out the Doctrine and Covenants which I had with me and I read to him this section: "Reproving betimes with sharpness, when moved upon by the Holy Ghost. . . ."

He said, "That's it. Where did that come from?"

I said, "That came from one of the revelations given to the Prophet of this last dispensation, Joseph Smith." It was hard for him to accept the source, but he gladly accepted the substance of that great revelation. That revelation itself defines the method by which counsel and reproof may be given and accepted by the people for their good. [*Stephen L Richards* 4]

Repentance

Innocent and "Presumptuous" Sin. In this connection I should like to call to your mind that under the old system of sacrifice, practiced in Israel, there was only one kind of sin for which they could offer sacrifice and through the sacrifice gain forgiveness, and that was the sin done innocently.

But for the sin that was done, as they said, "presumptuously," sin done deliberately, after planning, there was no ritual, it is said, provided in the great Mosaic Law by which forgiveness could be obtained for that. That stood between them and their God.

And I am wondering whether or not there is not something still left of that principle with us. I am wondering if the man who plots his sin, whatever it may be, stands in the same position as the man who sins innocently. I would hate, personally, to assume that I should so stand. Premeditation, deliberation, planning, gives a character to sin that is not possessed by one who sins innocently.

Now I would like to say this, please do not feel that you may go forward without much trouble, do a little sinning here, a little sinning there, and then after a while when you get tired, or for some, too old, repent and be saved and exalted. I am not sure that I know just what repentance is, how it works, any more than I am sure I know just what faith is, any more than I am sure I perceive all the intricacies related to baptism. There are some things we take on faith, and I take those on faith. I am not sure I understand them. But I do not want to take any chances. [*J. Reuben Clark, Jr.* 4]

Mercy and Justice. The Lord warns and forewarns us of our errors and miscalculation. He calls us mercifully to repentance, to abide his laws that he may give us the blessings predicated thereon. When we do not repent, we really have no claim on mercy because repentance is the price fixed therefor. How wonderful it is that we are all on the same plane; we must all pay for what we get. The price is fair, and justice is the result. [*Henry D. Moyle* 4]

Profit from Mistakes. The mistakes and inadequacies of the past, sorrowfully and repentantly remembered, need not be continually, insidiously destructive of our personal peace and of our possibilities for contribution and service. They should trouble us only with that trouble which will keep us humble and repentant and alert against any repetition of the sin. [*Marion D. Hanks* 3]

The gospel as I understand it says to man that it doesn't matter a whole lot what you have been, if today you decide to be something else, and that something comes more nearly to being what you can be. [*Marion D. Hanks* 2]

Retracing Steps. Beginnings are very important. They are important in the choice of professions, in all the decisions of life, in the choice of a lifetime companion. The beginnings of habits are important. The beginning of every venture in life, the first step in any direction, is tremendously important. . . .

If you have made some bad beginnings and taken some steps in the wrong direction, don't ever suppose that because you have taken one, that it is all right to take another, or that you have to take another. The quicker you step back from a wrong step, the less ground you are going to have to retrace, the less time you are going to lose, the less apology you are going to have to make, the less sorrow you are going to have. But always remember the great and blessed principle of repentance, if and when you need it—and do your best to avoid needing it. [*Richard L. Evans* 2]

"Except Ye Become as a Child." We may love God as a child does if we are willing to become submissive and surrender our hearts to him as a child does, not surrendering integrity or initiative or intelligence, but growing in these things through search and study and diligent effort.

I learned an important lesson from my children when I walked into the kitchen one day and found my four-year-old daughter employing some visual aids as she instructed her three-year-old sister in the use of the butcher knife. Being a normal father, somewhat hopeful as to the future of the children, I interfered and attempted to explain the seriousness of this adventure, but seemed not to get through to her. So I did what this little girl dislikes above all things, being a free soul; I stood her in the corner, and she sobbed and sobbed and said for the first time in her life, "You don't love me."

Well, she was wrong, but she stood there weeping, and this first important lesson of two that came out of the incident occurred. Father was disciplining Susan, and her little sister, the object of much of her bossism and torment and errand-sending, came on the scene. Here was her tormentor weeping in the corner at the mercy of father. What did she do, get a stick and help me beat her? Not at all; she went over and stood with her and put her arms around her and wept with her, and they both looked at me like I was an ogre. What a lesson! If, in fact, father is disciplining some, if in fact some (as each of us must) are learning lessons which will equip them eternally for further blessings, what is the obligation we have toward them? To get a stick and help beat them? Not for a minute. The obligation is to put our arms around them and lift them as best we can to the highest level of their possibilities, which in the ultimate may be higher than our own, if we are not as diligent as they.

This lesson, a lesson of love and mercy and compassion,

a lesson of real understanding, at age three, is a lesson I have profited from greatly.

May I tell you that there is great symbolism in a little child's putting her arms around someone in trouble, and loving her and weeping with her. This has a lot to do with the love of God and the love of brother, and that has a lot to do with anyone's achieving his highest spiritual possibilities. Without it there are some words the Lord used that apply: "Sounding brass, tinkling cymbals, whited sepulchres, etc."

One other lesson: when this little incident in the corner finished, we had quite a talk with these two little ones about our feeling toward them and our relationship to them. At four the next morning we heard them in the next room talking. The three-year-old had had a bad dream and had gone to crawl in with her sister to be comforted. The four-year-old said to the three-year-old the sweetest things I believe I have ever heard in this world. She said, "Nancy, do you know that Mommy and Daddy love us, even when we are naughty? They're 'dist trying to teach us."

Could I tell you how important that knowledge is to your life? This is more than a childish lesson. This is a lesson without which no one may understand the gospel to live it or share it, I believe. There are all around us wonderful people who have every reason to hope for happiness and fulfillment, and who are lost to their possibilities because they will not believe that God loves them even when they are naughty, and will forgive them, and forget, and never mention their mistakes, if, in humility, they repent, which (the Lord said to the Prophet) means to confess their sins and forsake them. [*Marion D. Hanks* 1]

Our Responsibility to Forgive.   A few years ago a boy came into class. [In the Utah State Prison] After class he said, "Brother Smith, can I talk to you for a minute?" We went into the old library where we could be alone. He said, "My name is Jim Jones. I am from a small town up north." And then he started to cry as I have never seen a man cry in my life. His whole body shook with sobs. When he could control himself he said, "What have I done? What have I done to my parents, to my Church, to my town?" He said, "My dad is superintendent of the Mutual in my home town; my mother is a teacher in the Sunday School. Why the bishop used to hold me up as an example to the boys of the ward and say, 'Why can't you be like Jim?' " Then this boy said, "What have I done?"

I said, "Jim, you are going to be here for some time. I hope you will come and study with us. I hope you will come to Church and take advantage of the time you have here." And he did. A year and a half passed, and the parole board said, "You can go back home on the thirteenth of November on parole"—three months distant.

That night as we went into the prison, he came up to me and said, "Ray, what am I going to do now?"

I said, "What are you going to do? This is the day we have waited for. You are going home on the thirteenth of November."

He said, "I can't go home. I am ashamed to go home. I have brought disgrace to my parents. My home town is just a little town; everyone there knows everyone else. What am I going to do?"

He was only a young fellow—nineteen years of age.

I wrote to the bishop of Jim's home town. I said, "Bishop, on the thirteenth of November, Jim Jones of your ward is going to be released from the Utah State Prison. I want to come down and talk in sacrament meeting the following Sunday, if you have an opening."

The bishop graciously wrote back and said, "The time is yours."

That Sunday my wife and I got in the car and started down for Jim's home. On the way she said, "This is a long way to go to Church." On the way back she said, "It was worth it."

We arrived about an hour early, found the family, had a little lunch with them. About a quarter to seven Jim started walking back and forth, fixing his tie, wondering, "What will happen? What will they say when they see me in Church? They all know where I have been."

Well, we went over to the chapel. I sat on the stand with the bishop, of course. The people came in; they filled the seats; they filled the aisles; they sat in the back. The bishop looked at me and said, "I don't know what has happened. We don't have a crowd like this even at conference." And he said, "All I said last Sunday was that a man from the penitentiary was going to bring one of our boys home."

I was very happy that all of the townspeople were there. I had something to say to them that night. "You know I believe that when a criminal goes to prison and those doors clang shut on him, they should stay shut forever. They should never open. He should die in prison. There is no place for a criminal outside of prison walls." I made that statement in the meeting that night. Then I said, "Jim, will you stand please?" And this boy stood up and all eyes of his neighbors turned to look at him. I said, "Brothers and sisters, a year and a half ago this boy came to us in the Utah State Prison, branded as a criminal, convicted of a crime against the people of the State of Utah. I saw that criminal die. And this boy I am bringing back to you is not a criminal. He is just a humble, repentant boy, who wants another chance in his home town to prove that he is decent. I have brought him back home through the front door of your Church. Now if you don't want him here, he will find companionship in the pool halls and the beer parlors, and after about three months I will have him back in prison again. Now it is all up to you."

It was a wonderful sight, brothers and sisters, when that meeting was over, to see the townspeople gather around that family. No wonder that on our way home the wife said it was worth it. [*Ray F. Smith*]

Revelation

Individual Revelation. As one of the humblest among you, and occupying the station I do, I want to bear you my humble testimony that I have received by the voice and the power of revelation, the knowledge and an understanding that God is.

It was a week following the Conference when I was preparing myself for a radio talk on the Life of the Savior, when I read again the story of the life, the crucifixion and the resurrection of the Master, there came to me as I read that, the reality of that story. More than just what was on the written page. For in truth, I felt as if I were viewing the scenes with a certainty as though I had been there in person. I know that these things come by the revelations of the living God.

I bear you my solemn testimony that we live in the Church today that has revelation. Every soul in it who has been blessed to receive the Holy Ghost has the power to receive revelation. God help you and me that we will always so live that the Lord can answer the prayers of the faithful through us in our good deeds. [*Harold B. Lee* 1]

Understanding Prophecy. When the Lord opens our understandings so that by the power of the Holy Ghost, the power by which prophecy was uttered, we are able to understand prophecy; then prophecy becomes a guide to us and is a more sure word than anything we can find in the world. [*LeGrand Richards* 3]

Inspiration. There is much revelation other than the open vision and the spoken word. There is revelation which comes into the mind, without the aid of the ear. This type of revelation I know a little about from personal experience. I have never seen an open vision. I'm not sure that I have ever heard the spoken voice of a divine person. I have, however, received revelation which came into my mind. For example, one time I was speaking at a funeral. I didn't know the children of the deceased mother whose funeral we were holding. Thinking I had finished my remarks, I turned as if to close and sit down, when through my mind there went a sentence, "Turn around and bear your testimony." I turned around and bore my testimony. I bore it with more fervor, vigor and clarity than I have the power, of myself, to bear it. When I was through, I didn't know why I had done it.

I had no intimation as to why for over a year. Then one day a woman from Idaho came to see me. She had been acquainted with one of the daughters of the woman for whom the funeral was held. Upon returning to Idaho from the funeral of her mother, this daughter immediately began to take a great interest in the Church. Upon inquiry as to the cause of her changed life, the daughter said, "I went to Salt Lake to the funeral of my mother. I thought we were having an ordinary funeral, when one of the speakers, who I thought had finished, suddenly turned around and bore his testimony. And that testimony," she said "went into my heart like fire. I was convinced that I should return to the faith of my mother." [*Marion G. Romney* 4]

Revealed to a Child. I have a believing heart because of a simple testimony that came when I was a child, I think maybe I was around ten—maybe eleven—years of age. I was with my father out on a farm away from home. Over the fence from our place were some tumbledown sheds which had attracted a curious boy, adventurous as I was. I started to climb through the fence and I heard a voice as clearly as you are hearing mine—"Don't go over there!" calling me by name. I turned to look where father was working to see if he were talking to me, but he was way up at the other end of the field. There was no person in sight. I realized then, as a child, that there were persons beyond my sight and I had heard a voice. And when I had heard and read these stories of the Prophet Joseph Smith, I, too, knew what it meant to hear a voice because I had heard from an unseen speaker. [*Harold B. Lee* 1]

Revelation in New Zealand. I remember when President Rufus K. Hardy, of the First Council of Seventy, passed away. I was walking along the street of one of the cities in New Zealand, and one of our native members came up —a lady.

She said to me, "President Hardy is dead."

I said, "Is that so? Have you received a wire?"

She said, "No. I received a message, but I haven't received any wire." She repeated, "He's dead. I know."

Well, I always believed them when they told me those things. When I got back to headquarters, here came a cablegram which said that President Hardy passed away the night before. But she knew that without any cablegram.

* * *

She told me about it.

After President Hardy died we had a memorial service for him. I'll never forget the native who was up speaking, saying what a calamity it was to the mission to lose this great New Zealand missionary who could do so much for them as one of the authorities of the Church. He was talking along that line, and all of a sudden he stopped and he looked around at me and said, "Wait a minute. There's nothing to worry about. Not a thing to worry about. When President Cowley gets home he'll fill the first vacancy in the Council of the Twelve Apostles, and we'll still have a representative among the authorities of the Church." Then he went on talking about President Hardy. When I arrived home the following September I filled the first vacancy in the Quorum of the Twelve. [*Matthew Cowley* 1]

Keeping in Tune. Some years ago when I served as a stake president, we had a very grievous case that had to come before the high council and the stake presidency which resulted in the excommunication of a man who had harmed a lovely young girl. After nearly an all-night session which resulted in that action, I went to my office rather weary the next morning, to be confronted by a brother of this man whom we had had on trial the night before. This man said, "I want to tell you that my brother wasn't guilty of that thing which you charged him with."

"How do you know he wasn't guilty?" I asked.

"Because I prayed, and the Lord told me he was innocent," the man answered. I asked him to come into the office and we sat down, and I asked, "Would you mind if I ask you a few personal questions?" and he said, "Certainly not."

"How old are you."

"Forty-seven."

"What priesthood do you hold?"

He said he thought he was a teacher.

"Do you keep the Word of Wisdom?"

He said, "Well, no." He used tobacco, which was obvious.

"Do you pay your tithing?"

He said, "No"—and he didn't intend to as long as that blankety-blank-blank man was the bishop of the Thirty-second Ward.

I said, "Do you attend your priesthood meetings?"

He replied, "No sir!" and he didn't intend to as long as that man was bishop. "You don't attend your sacrament meetings either?"

"No, sir."

"Do you have your family prayers?"

And he said, "No."

"Do you study the scriptures?"

He said, "Well, my eyes are bad and I can't read very much."

I then said to him: "In my home I have a beautiful instrument called a radio. When everything is in good working order we can dial it to a certain station and pick up a speaker or the voice of a singer all the way across the continent or sometimes on the other side of the world, bringing them into the front room as though they were almost speaking there. But, after we had used it for a long time, there were some little delicate instruments or electrical devices on the inside called radio tubes that began to wear out. When one of them wears out, we get a kind of a static—it isn't so clear. . . . If we don't give that attention, and another one wears out—well, the radio sits there looking quite like it did before, but something has happened on the inside. We can't get any singer. We can't get any speaker.

"Now," I said, "you and I have within our souls something like what might be said to be a counter-part of those radio tubes. We might have what we call a 'Go-to-Sacrament-Meeting' tube, 'Keep-the-Word-of-Wisdom' tube, 'Read-the-Scriptures' tube, and, as one of the most important, that might be said to be the master tube of the whole soul, we might call the 'Keep-Yourselves-Morally-Clean' tube. If one of these becomes worn out by disuse or is not active—we fail to keep the commandments of God—it has the same effect upon our spiritual selves that that same worn out instrument in the radio in my home had upon the reception that we otherwise could receive from a distance.

"Now, then," I said, "fifteen of the best living men in the Pioneer Stake prayed last night. They heard the evidence and every man was united in saying that your brother was guilty. Now, you, who do none of these things, you say you prayed, and you got an opposite answer. How would you explain that?"

Then this man gave an answer that I think was a classic. He said, "Well, President Lee, I think I must have gotten my answer from the wrong source." And you know that's just as great a truth as we can have. We get our answer from the source of the power we list to obey. If we're keeping the commandments of the Devil, we'll get the answer from the Devil. If we're keeping the commandments of God, we'll get the commandments from our Heavenly Father for our direction and for our guidance. [*Harold B. Lee* 1]

Sacrament

From the time of Adam, two sacred ordinances have been instituted by the Lord to keep his people in remembrance of the Christ, the debt he was to pay, and the debt he did pay to redeem them from the effects of the fall.

First was the ordinance rite of sacrifice, which required offering the firstlings of the flocks which were to be without spot or blemish as a blood sacrifice to remind the people of the great sacrifice that the Son of God, who was also without spot or blemish, was to make to atone for the sins of men and to redeem them from the effects of Adam's fall. . . .

From Adam to Christ, the offering of sacrifice was a sacred rite of great spiritual significance and faithfully performed throughout the generations of Israel. Its purpose was to keep the covenant people of the Lord always in remembrance of the great sacrifice that Christ was to make upon the cross. The law of blood sacrifice was fulfilled in the sacrifice of Christ's life on Calvary.

The second ordinance instituted by the Christ was the ordinance of the sacrament which was introduced to his disciples in connection with the Last Supper. Now perhaps we should define what a sacrament is. A sacrament is a sacred, binding oath of allegiance to obey one's leader and not to desert his standard. Therefore, in partaking of the sacrament, we should always remember that it is a sacred binding oath of allegiance to obey our leader, who is Christ, and not to desert his standard of the gospel, which the

Apostle Paul taught was the power of God unto salvation. This definition we should always remember when we partake of the sacramental emblems.

The sacrament of the Lord is, therefore, a solemn religious ceremony instituted by Christ and involves a sacred obligation on the part of his disciples. [*Delbert L. Stapley* 2]

Service

Rewards of Service. Jesus and the prophets have spoken strongly against much or loud praying done for the sake of being heard by men; against fastings to be seen by men; against payment of tithes and offerings for the plaudits of men. In each case they have their reward, the seeing and hearing and plaudits of men. But this is not real worship or real service or real contribution, but only selfish and empty exhibitionism.

Development, growth, understanding . . . the *gaining* of our lives . . . come only as we lose our lives in honest love for God, for his work, for his children, expressed in obedience to him and in unselfish interest in them and service to them. [*Marion D. Hanks* 3]

Service to God and Man. Now the gospel of Jesus Christ establishes a most significant relationship between service to God and service to neighbor. It makes them one and the same thing. This may to some seem anomalous, but it is nevertheless true that a service to one's fellows is accepted by the Lord as a service to him personally. [*Marion G. Romney* 5]

Spiritual Gifts

The Blind Shall See. I've told the story about the little baby nine months old who was born blind. The father came up with him one Sunday and said, "Brother Cowley, our baby hasn't been blessed yet, we'd like you to bless him."

I said, "Why have you waited so long?"

"Oh, we just didn't get around to it."

Now, that's the native way; I like that. Just don't get around to doing things. Why not live and enjoy it. I said, "All right, what's the name?"

So he told me the name, and I was just going to start when he said, "By the way, give him his vision when you give him a name. He was born blind."

Well, it shocked me, but then I said to myself, "Why not? Christ said to his disciples when he left them, 'Greater things than I have done shall you do.'" And I had faith in that father's faith. After I gave that child its name, I finally got around to giving it its vision. That boy's about twelve years old now. The last time I was back there I was afraid to inquire about him. I was sure he had gone blind again. That's the way my faith works sometimes. So I asked the branch president about him. And he said, "Brother Cowley, the worst thing you ever did was to bless that child to receive his vision. He's the meanest kid in this neighborhood. Always getting into mischief." Boy, I was thrilled about that kid getting into mischief! [*Matthew Cowley* 1]

The Faith of Parents. A little over a year ago a couple came into my office carrying a little boy. The father said to me, "My wife and I have been fasting for two days, and we've brought our little boy up for a blessing. You are the one we've been sent to."

I said, "What's the matter with him?"

They said he was born blind, deaf and dumb, no co-ordination of his muscles, couldn't even crawl at the age of five years. I said to myself, this is it. "This kind cometh not out save by fasting and by prayer." I had implicit faith in the fasting and the prayers of those parents. I blessed that child, and a few weeks later I received a letter: "Brother Cowley, we wish you could see our little boy now. He's crawling. When we throw a ball across the floor he races after it on his hands and knees. He can see. When we clap our hands over his head he jumps. He can hear." Medical science had laid the burden down. God had taken over. The little boy was rapidly recovering, or really getting what he'd never had. [*Matthew Cowley* 1]

Fasting and Prayer. I have a friend down in Honolulu. He was called one day to the hospital by one of our native sisters who had a child there with polio. She said, "Bishop, hurry up to the hospital and give my child a blessing." That was one morning. He never showed up all day. The next afternoon he went up, and she started giving him a tongue lashing. "You, my bishop, your own boss. I asked you to come and bless my child seriously ill, and you didn't show up."

He waited until she had finished and then he said, "When I hung up the receiver yesterday I started to fast. I've been fasting and praying. Now I'm ready." That was early in the afternoon. He blessed the child. The child went home that evening, released from the hospital. "This kind cometh not out save by fasting and by prayer." [*Matthew Cowley* 1]

Except Ye Believe as a Child. A few weeks ago I was called to the County Hospital in Salt Lake City by a mother.

I didn't know her. She said her boy was dying from polio and asked if I would come down and give that boy a blessing. So I picked up a young bishop whom I generally take with me, for I think his faith is greater than mine, and I always like him along. We went down there and here was this young lad in an iron lung, unconscious, his face rather a blackish color, with a tube in his throat, and they said he had one lower down in his abdomen. He had been flown in from an outlying community. The mother said to me, "This is an unusual boy. Not because he's my child, but he is an unusual boy." I think he was eight or nine years of age.

After they put the usual coverings on us we went in and we blessed the boy. It was one of those occasions when I knew as I laid my hands upon that lad he was an unusual boy, and that he had faith. Having faith in his faith, I blessed him to get well and promised him he would. I never heard any more about him until last Saturday. I was on my way to Murray to conference; I dropped in the County Hospital, and I asked if I might see the lad. The nurse said, "Certainly. Walk right down the hall." As I walked down the hall, out came the boy running to meet me. He ran up and asked, "Are you Brother Cowley?"

And I said, "Yes."

He said, "I want to thank you for that prayer." He added, "I was unconscious then, wasn't I?"

I replied, "You certainly were."

He said, "That's the reason I don't recognize you." Then he asked, "Come on in my room; I want to talk to you." He was an unusual boy. Well, we went in the room. He still had a tube in his throat. I said, "How long are you going to have that tube there?"

He said, "Oh, two weeks. Two more weeks and then I'm all well. How about another blessing?"

So I said, "Certainly." I blessed him again, and then I was in a hurry. I wanted to get out to my conference. But he stopped me and asked, "Hey, how about my partner in the next bed?" There was a young fellow about sixteen or seventeen.

I said, "What do you mean?"

He said, "Don't go out without blessing him. He's my partner."

I said, "Sure." Then I asked the boy, "Would you like a blessing?"

He said, "Yes, sir. I'm a teacher in the Aaronic Priesthood in my ward." I blessed him, and then my little friend went and brought another fellow in. Here was another partner. And I blessed him.

Now, except ye believe as a child, you can't receive these blessings. We have to have the faith of a child in order to believe in these things, especially when you reach college age and your minds are so full of skepticism and doubt. I guess there are some things that you should doubt. But you can become as a little child in these things. Miracles are commonplace, brothers and sisters. [*Matthew Cowley* 1]

Healing the Sick.   I went into a hospital one day in New Zealand to bless a woman who didn't belong to the Church. She was dying. We all knew she was dying. The doctor even said so. She was having her farewell party. Ah, that's one thing I like about the natives. When you go they give you a farewell party. They all gather around. They send messages over to the other side. "When you get over there tell my mother I'm trying to do my best; I'm not so good, but I'm trying."

"Tell her to have a good room fixed for me when I get over there—plenty of fish, good meals."

My, it's wonderful how they send you off. Well, there they were, all gathered around this poor sister. She was about to be confined, and the doctor told her it would kill her. She was tubercular from head to foot. I had with me an old native, almost ninety. She was his niece. He stood up at the head of the bed and he said, "Vera, you're dead. You're dead because the doctor says you're dead. You're on your way out. I've been to you, your home and your people, my relatives. I'm the only one that joined the Church. None of you has ever listened to me. You're dead now, but you're going to live." He turned to me and said, "Is it all right if we kneel down and pray?"

I said, "Yes." So we knelt down. Everybody around there knelt down. And after the prayer we blessed her. The last time I was in New Zealand she had had her fifth child, physically well from head to foot. She has not joined the Church yet. That's the next miracle I'm waiting for. [*Matthew Cowley* 1]

Raising the Dead. I was called to a home in a little village in New Zealand one day. There the Relief Society sisters were preparing the body of one of our Saints. They had placed his body in front of the big house, as they call it, the house where the people came to wail and weep and mourn over the dead, when in rushed the dead man's brother.

He said, "Administer to him."

And the young natives said, "Why, you shouldn't do that; he's dead."

"You do it!"

This same old man that I had with me when his niece was so ill, was there. The younger native got down on his knees and he anointed this man. Then this great old sage got down and blessed him and commanded him to rise. You should have seen the Relief Society sisters scatter. And he sat up and he said, "Send for the elders; I don't feel very well." . . . Well, we told him he had just been administered to, and he said, "Oh, that was it." He said, "I was dead. I could feel life coming back into me just like a blanket unrolling." Now, he outlived the brother that came in and told us to administer to him. [*Matthew Cowley* 1]

The Lame Shall Walk. I was down on the Indian reservation when I met a sister who had just joined the Church, a beautiful Navajo woman. My they dress beautifully down there. I've never seen an immodestly dressed woman, never seen any indecent exposure in any Indian. Beautiful velvet dresses. . . . Modesty—my it's wonderful. It's wonderful to be modest. They get on these beautiful dresses and go out and buy their groceries at the trading post. Anyway, after I'd met this sister one of the missionaries called me off to the side and said, "A few months ago my companion and I went into a hogan and that lady, that Indian sister, was lying on the ground on a sheepskin. She had been lying there for six long years. We called on her, and when we were leaving she called us back and said in broken English, 'Isn't there something you do for sick people?' "

And we said, "Yes."

She said, "Please do it for me." So they got down on their knees and administered to her, by the authority of the priesthood and in the name of Jesus Christ. Then they left, and they weren't away fifty yards when she came out of the hogan after them and said, "Come back and see what you have done for me." She walked. God does have control of all of these elements. You and I can reach out, and if it's his will we can bring those elements under our control for his purposes. [*Matthew Cowley* 1]

Interpretation of Tongues. The occasion was a conference held at Huntly, New Zealand — a thousand people assembled. Before that time I had spoken through interpreters in China, Hawaii, and other places, but I felt impressed on that occasion to speak in the English language. In substance I said, "I have never been much of an advocate of the necessity of tongues in our Church, but today I wish I had that gift. But I haven't. However, I am going to speak to you, my brethren and sisters, in my native tongue and pray that you may have the gift of interpretation of tongues. We shall ask Brother Meha, who has been asked to interpret for me, to make notes and if necessary he may give us a summary of my talk afterwards."

Well, the outpouring of the gift of tongues on that occasion was most remarkable. Following the end of my sermon, Brother Sid Christy, a Maori student of the Brigham Young University who had returned to New Zealand, rushed up to me following the sermon, and said: "Brother McKay, they got your message!"

I knew the people had received my message by the attention and the nodding of their heads during the talk. I said, "I think they have, but for the benefit of those who may not have understood, or had the gift, we shall have the sermon interpreted."

While Brother Meha was interpreting or giving a summary of the speech in the Maori language, some of the natives, who had understood it, but who did not understand English, arose and corrected him in his interpretation.

President George Albert Smith and Brother Rufus K. Hardy visited New Zealand several years after that event and Brother Hardy, hearing of the event, brought home written testimonies of those who were present and he took the occasion to have these testimonies notarized. So it was the gift of interpretation rather than the gift of tongues that was remarkable. [David O. McKay 1]

Karl G. Maeser had prayed and yearned for some testimony to be given to him at the time of his baptism, some spiritual manifestation. Writing of that desire, he later said:

On coming out of the water, I lifted both of my hands to heaven and said, 'Father, if what I have done just now is pleasing unto thee, give me a testimony, and whatever thou shouldst require of my hands I shall do, even to the laying down of my life for this cause.'

At first there seemed to be no response to his fervent appeal, and he walked home together with President Richards and Elder Budge, one on the right and one on the left, and they conversed about the power of the priesthood. Then a most extraordinary thing occurred, one of the great evidences of spiritual power in our dispensation. President Richards could speak and understand no German. Karl G. Maeser could neither speak nor understand English. William Budge was acting as interpreter. But suddenly, so Karl G. Maeser tells us, when President Richards was speaking English he understood him clearly, fully. And suddenly, likewise, when Karl G. Maeser was speaking German, President Richards understood him clearly and fully. And so they conversed for the remainder of the walk home, without the need for an interpreter. Then, so Karl G. Maeser tells us, the power as suddenly left as it had come. He bore testimony:

This is the plain statement of the power of the Holy Spirit manifested to me by the mercy of my Heavenly Father, the first one of the many that have followed and that have corroborated the sincere conviction of my soul, that the Church of Jesus Christ of Latter-day Saints is of God and not of man.

[*Bruce B. Clark*]

Temple Work

Importance of Temples. We look upon temples as the most important and priceless buildings in all the world. Why? Because only in temples can we obtain God's greatest blessing of *eternal life*. It is possible to go into many famed schools throughout the nation and in other countries and obtain degrees of varying value. But to obtain the highest degree of the celestial kingdom, to be blessed with eternal life, God's greatest gift to man, one must go to the only place in the world where that degree can be obtained, the temple of the Lord. And so, a temple becomes the most important building in all the world—a connecting link between heaven and earth. [*Archibald F. Bennett*]

The Family, an Eternal Unit. . . . you may have all seen the show or read the book, *A Man Called Peter*. I had the privilege of spending an hour, or an hour and a half, with Peter in his study in Atlanta when he was occupying the pulpit in the Presbyterian Church. I asked him what was the attitude of his church with respect to eternal marriage and the eternal duration of the family unit.

"Well," he said, "Mr. Richards, we are not allowed to teach that doctrine in our church." I knew that they were not, because I had their own statement for it. "But," he said, "in my own mind, I have stubborn objections." And then he proceeded with this explanation. "When you take the kitten away from the cat, in a few days, the cat has forgotten all about the kitten. When you take the calf away from the cow, in a few days the cow has forgotten all about the calf. But when you take a child away from its mother's bosom, though she live to be one hundred years old, she never forgets the child of her bosom. I find it difficult to believe that God created love like that to perish in the grave." [*LeGrand Richards* 5]

Universal Salvation. When I was in Holland, I was invited one night to speak to a Bible Class in the Hague at the home of a prominent furniture dealer. I was asked to speak on the subject of "Universal Salvation," which includes the preaching of the gospel in the spirit world, and baptizing for the dead—the opportunity that God has prepared for those who do not hear the gospel here in mortality to hear it and to accept it. They gave me an hour and a half, twenty of them sitting around the room, all with their Bibles, and as far as I can remember, not one question was asked me during the entire time. I just proceeded to explain to them the glorious truths recorded in their own scriptures. And when I was through I closed my Bible, laid it on the table, folded my arms and waited for a comment. The first comment came from the daughter of the man of the house. She said, "Father, I just can't understand. I have never attended one of these Bible classes in my life that you haven't had the last word to say on everything and tonight you haven't said a word."

He shook his head and said, "My daughter, there isn't anything to say. This man has been teaching us things we have never heard of, and he has been teaching them to us out of our own Bibles."

That is what the Lord meant when he said that this prophet [Joseph Smith] who would be great in his eyes should not only bring forth his word but that he would bring them to a conviction of his word, which had already gone forth among them. . . . [*LeGrand Richards* 5]

Testimony

Testimony and Church Standards. Development of a testimony of the truthfulness of the gospel of Jesus Christ is the greatest single factor in a sound background for meeting the world and maintaining one's Church standards. [*Milan D. Smith*]

Steps Necessary to Obtain a Testimony. There are certain definite steps you have to take to get a testimony. . . . You have to believe in Jesus Christ, that he is the Son of God. You have to repent of your sins. You have to be baptized by water and also by the imposition of hands for the Holy Ghost, and then you have to continue in obedience to the principles of the gospel. [*Marion G. Romney 1*]

The Holy Ghost Gives Testimony. A testimony never comes to a person through the learning of the world; man's learning doesn't get it. You cannot get it through philosophizing or through the study of what men have said who did not have a testimony. . . . A testimony has to come through the Holy Ghost. Any person who ever had a testimony had it because it had been given to him by the inspiration of the Holy Ghost. [*Marion G. Romney 1*]

"The Church and the Kingdom of God First." Then I had a call to go to California and preside over a stake. People did not know it, but the President of the Church sent my father over to my office to see how I would like to go down there, and I said, "Well, father, I do not know what I would do for a living down there. I have ten men and two girls working for me, and they depend upon me for a living. And my children are just at the mating age, and I would not like to take them away from their friends. You had better tell the President that I do not know what I would do for a living, but I love the Church enough to go anywhere it wants me to, and if he wants me to go I will go down and look around."

And the President said, "Tell him to go look around," and in sixty days we had sold our business and had moved to California. Again, this is what my testimony did for me. [*LeGrand Richards* 4]

I think now of . . . Brother Benson. You all know him. When he was called to be a member of the Twelve, nothing was said to him about whether he would get an allowance to live on, and I was back in his stake to attend a conference. I knew him well, and he said, "LeGrand, do they make any provision for the General Authorities to live?"

"Well," I said, "they give you a living allowance, but you will not live like you are living here unless you have something tucked away that you can draw on." I happened to know that Brother Benson had an offer for just about ten times as much per month as the allowance that the brethren gave him. Why did he not take that offer of ten times as much? Because of his testimony. . . "the Church and the Kingdom of God first" as President Taylor used to say, and so you know what happened. [*LeGrand Richards* 4]

When I chose Bishop Isaacson to be my counselor in the Presiding Bishopric, his tithing had been just about the same each year as his allowance is now as a member of the Presiding Bishopric. In fact, when he got his first six months' checks he turned them right into the cashier and said, "Credit these back, I have never been on a mission, it is about time I am doing something for the Church." When President George Albert Smith asked him, in my presence, if he would be willing to serve as my counselor, thinking of that fine business he had, he said, "Yes, President Smith, but I would like to go back to South Bend, Indiana, to see if the president of our company will let me appoint a manager, so I can save some of my business. You know, in the insurance business so much of it is renewals, and you receive in the future the reward of your labors of the past." "But," he said, "if they will not let me do it, I will tell them to take the business." [*LeGrand Richards* 4]

Testimony from a Child. I will not forget the night when a fine, mature, successful, affluent man stood in a large congregation and bore his witness. It was a witness that testified to me what the thirty-second chapter of Alma also testifies and what my own experience has testified: that testimony and conviction and assurance and confidence about the truth can come with earnest search and the living of the life at whatever age.

The man told of his little boy who at age eight came to his bedside with a message. The man had been for seventeen years a cynical, critical, quite heartless antagonist of his wife and children who were members of the Church. His business partner was a Latter-day Saint bishop who found his life somewhat difficult because of this man's attitude. The man went on in his criticism through the years, while his wife, in spite of his problem behavior, dedicated herself and her children to the Church. The time came when this man, having suffered a broken back in an automobile accident, lay in bed for months. His little boy came and announced that he was going to be baptized, and said, "Daddy I wish you could be with me."

The man had mellowed a little under the circumstances of his recent experience. He said, "I wish I could too, son, but you come and tell me about it when you get home."

The little boy came back. He said, "Daddy, I have been wanting to talk to you for a long time, and I'm going to do it now. I have just been baptized into the Church. You are a wonderful Daddy, and I love you very much but this is what I want to say to you: I have only been on this earth eight years, and I know that the gospel is true. You've been here forty-eight years and you don't know that it is true yet, and the reason is that you don't really want to. You won't read the books Mother has tried to get you to read; you won't listen to the missionaries or the teachers. You could know, but you just don't want to."

The little boy went on his way, and this mature, successful, influential citizen lay and wept and, according to his own account, acknowledged the charge. When he got on his feet again he continued to do what he had started to do while in bed, to pay the price of learning. He "searched diligently," and stood before us as an active stake missionary with some very successful adventures in service, to testify through tears and great emotion that he did now know the gospel was true. [*Marion D. Hanks*]

A Testimony Renewed. I just recently read of the testimony of my great grandfather on my mother's side to his large family before his passing. All his family gathered around him. He wanted to deliver to them his last testimony of the restoration of this work, of his knowledge and his intimacy with the Prophet Joseph Smith, and he said something like this:

My children, I have guarded the Prophet Joseph Smith while he slept; I have guarded him while he walked in the earth. I have slept at his side. I have felt the power of God in his life. I have seen the mantle of the Holy Ghost hover over him. I have received the witness that I know that he is and he was a Prophet of the living God, and I want you children, my family to honor him and to honor each succeeding prophet following him, because your security in the kingdom of God and your security in the Church depends upon your full allegiance in the Prophets in the earth. This testimony I leave with you, and I know that he was, indeed a Prophet of the living God.

My fellow students, a testimony is a great thing. It starts in early youth and remains even though sometimes dormant. I heard a man bear his testimony the other day which I would like to leave with you. I called upon him extemporaneously to the stand, and he said:

> This is the first time in thirty years that I have stood to bear my testimony. I want to bear witness of something within my heart.

Then he told how he was an adopted son, and had been taken in a home where he had not been properly treated. He knew not his mother and father, and he said:

> I saw the other children were favored, and there began to develop in my heart the spirit to kill. From a boy of ten until the time I was sixteen, I prayed every day of my life that I would have the power, the confidence and the strength to snuff the very existence and life from my stepfather.
>
> I waited and I developed my muscles. I walked out to the barn and chinned myself day and night to develop enough strength in my arms that when the time came, I could pounce upon him and smother him to death. The opportunity came, and I sprang upon him like a lion, and I dropped him to the ground. I sank my fingers deep into his throat. I saw his very life being snuffed out of him. Then I heard a voice say to me, "Don't kill him." I raised myself from over the body of my stepfather and stood there like a bear with my claws pointing towards his throat.
>
> Then he said, "I heard the voice of God."

That fellow became a wayward, careless man following that time, even though he had received this witness. Today this man has a beautiful family, is active in the Church. He is a man of God. He said in the closing instance of his testimony, "I knew as a youth that God lived. I was taught it in my Primary, but for thirty years this is the first time you have heard my voice. I thank God for my bishop who has brought me back to the Church." [*Wendell Mendenhall*]

Personal Testimonies. I testify to you out of the brief experience of my life, that while there are difficulties and problems, while there are hypocrisies and questionable performances among us, that all of those may be heaped on one side of the scale and will be outweighed immeasurably by this observable truth, that one who learns the gospel (that is, seeks earnestly and diligently to learn it), one who is prayerful and humble, who approaches affirmatively the problems that exist, who walks uprightly and seeks to remember his covenants—such a person is immeasurably happier than he otherwise has been or could be. [*Marion D. Hanks* 4]

. . . I know that God lives. I know that Jesus is the Christ. I know that Joseph Smith was a Prophet of God. And if there ever was a miracle in the history of mankind that miracle is this *Church,* which has grown to its present greatness in the earth. And your institution [BYU] stems from the prayer of a boy who was persecuted, who was driven from pillar to post, whose life was taken, who has been branded as the greatest fraud that ever lived on the American continent. This Church from that kind of a fraud is the greatest miracle of modern history. And it's a miracle of God our Father. May you all have an inward witness that Joseph Smith was a prophet, that God used him to bring about his purposes in this dispensation of the fullness of times. May we always be loyal, devoted and simple in our faith, I pray in the name of Jesus Christ. Amen. [*Matthew Cowley* 1]

I appeal to you to be true to the Church. I bear you testimony here today that God does live. He is our Father, literally the Father of our spirits. He lives. He is as much a reality as you are. He does live. He is a person and he is our Father. Jesus is the Christ, the Son of Almighty God. He is divine. He is the Redeemer of the world. He wrought out a great atonement for you. I bear you testimony that Joseph Smith was a prophet of the Lord in the same sense in which Moses was, or Abraham, Isaac, or Jacob or Isaiah or Jeremiah or Ezekiel or any other prophet that has ever lived on the earth. As the Doctrine and Covenants points out, he did more for the salvation of men than anybody else who ever lived in the earth with the sole exception of

Jesus Christ. As the instrument in the hands of God, Joseph Smith restored the true Church of Jesus Christ and I declare to you in all solemnity that this Church is true and that it is in fact the kingdom of God on this earth. And I testify to you that the Bible is true, the word of God, that the Book of Mormon is true, that the Doctrine and Covenants and the Pearl of Great Price are true, the word of God himself to you. [*Mark E. Petersen* 4]

Tithing

It's possible for everyone of us to learn how to pay our tithing, perfectly. It was only day before yesterday that I went to the bishop of my own ward on tithing settlement day. He is now retiring from his position as bishop to go out and preside over the Central States Mission. He said, "I want to bear you a testimony that I've gained in six years of experience as a bishop. In all of this time I have had hundreds and hundreds of full tithepayers come to report their tithing, and in all that time I have never had one of them approach me, throw down his check or his money and say, 'Well, there it is,' as though it were a terrible task, but they have all come happily because they felt they were doing the will of the Lord." The one who learns how to pay his tithing perfectly is a happy man. [*Harold B. Lee* 2]

Truth

Importance of Truth. . . . there is nothing quite so wonderful and so powerful and so eternal and so great as the truth. That is what gives us intelligence and power; that is what purifies us and eventually exalts us. . . . And the center truth of our lives is found in the gospel of Jesus Christ, in his atonement for the sins of the world, in his fulfilling of the mission given him by the Father to be the Redeemer of the world. . . . [*George Q. Morris* 3]

Education for Truth. It has been said that education is concerned with truth. Our major premise should be the necessity for free inquiry. However, both in school and throughout life, some of us should be engaged in creative activities, the products of which each one hopes will have significance for a long period of time. A scholar should be dedicated to the advancement of learning; his ambition must be, not to an immediate undertaking, but to a long range human enterprise. This will be particularly true in the lives of Latter-day Saints who have their sights set on a millennium. Their purposes day by day are spiritual as well as temporal. [*Henry D. Moyle* 5]

There is no realm of knowledge we are in any wise prohibited from exploring. It is all ours to procure. No law by which we are bound that we cannot discover if we seek and search diligently therefor. All truth is ours to acquire. [*Henry D. Moyle* 2]

In all matters pertaining to our welfare here and hereafter, freedom and power go hand in hand. Today, even in our own country, there is too marked a process of bringing everyone into agreement about things, the truth of which could best be that which is advanced by so-called leaders in their respective fields. The discovery of error is neither advanced by agreement or unity of thought. We might well discuss the disputes of previous generations to see in proper perspective how void the present world would be if all learning were unified. How progress would be stifled if unity of thought prevailed today! Absence of dissenters spells stagnation. Controversy is essential to a healthful condition in life and learning. Our life finds its purpose in a never ending trail to find what thoughts of the human brain are warranted and what are not. [*Henry D. Moyle* 5]

To test beliefs of various methods to find standards by which we can evaluate good and evil, to classify new ideas as a part of our cultural heritage or reject them as illusions of the mind, we must find our own standards. We must live as individuals, study as individuals and be individuals in fact. Can this be called the search for truth? It is the truth that will make us free—free to exercise our own free agency to the fullest extent—something we cannot do unless truth is ours, as it pertains to the subject matter of our decisions. [*Henry D. Moyle* 5]

Our mission is clear. It is to carry on the search for the ultimate truths and to put our powers of reason and conscience to the service of God and man. [*Henry D. Moyle* 5]

He has laid down this simple principle: If we will believe in him and keep his commandments, we shall know the truth. I do not know of any other way of knowing it. [*George Q. Morris* 3]

Truth Is Narrow. The truth is narrow. Error broadens out into a million paths, into unending controversy in doctrine.

Now where does the narrowness come in? Who is the narrower—a man who says he will not accept supernatural things but only what his reason tells him is true, or the man who says, "I accept all that my reason and knowledge of facts will tell me is true. I accept all in this little bit of sphere that man operates in, but I do more than that. I accept the revealed word of God—the truth that governs the universe!"

We believe in accepting revelation and we expect to continue to accept it. That is not narrowness; that is being broad in the truest sense, accepting all truth in man's narrow sphere and also truth in God's sphere—that comprehends all truth. [George Q. Morris 2]

One True Church. There is only one true Church. It is the Church of Jesus Christ of Latter-day Saints. We are not intolerant when we make that statement. We merely follow the pattern of Jesus Christ. We are not intolerant in that we do not interfere with the religious views or the religious practices of anybody else. We do not persecute anybody else because of their religious ideas. We are tolerant in that we allow all men to worship God according to the dictates of their own consciences, although we insist also that we be allowed the same privilege, for we understand thoroughly that there is only one way in which to be saved. There is nothing intolerant about that. [Mark E. Petersen 1]

Truth versus Ignorance. When we learn truth, then problems of bigotry and bitterness of hatred and intolerance and lack of understanding and arrogance and the attitude of superiority, these things disappear, for they are the products of ignorance. . . . [Marion D. Hanks 2]

Support Truth without Apology. Now I know that none of us wishes to appear to be arbitrary, dogmatic, in the bad sense. We don't need to be that way, but we do need to speak the truth, and in the true sense we can only be dogmatic. Truth is dogmatic. We must declare the revealed word of God upon which this Church stands, and we must speak it without hesitation and without apology. Never let any of us feel ashamed or embarrassed because people make fun of us and ridicule our doctrine. [*George Q. Morris* 2]

A simple truth: There is no salvation in man's power and knowledge and wisdom. [*George Q. Morris* 3]

The Holy Ghost Guides to Truth. Jesus pointed out to Nicodemus the steps by which he could, and every other child of God can, be born again, that is, have his understanding opened to the things of the Spirit. You, of course, know that these steps are the first principles and ordinances of the gospel—faith in the Lord Jesus Christ, repentance, baptism and reception of the Holy Ghost. If you will, by complying with these requirements, come into possession of and cultivate the gift of the Holy Ghost, the spirit of revelation, which is the learning process by which truth is divined, and if you will search the scriptures until you become acquainted with the store of divine knowledge recorded in them, you will possess the key by which the conclusions of men may be tested to see if they comport with that truth which is knowledge of things as they are, as they were, and as they are to come. [*Marion G. Romney* 6]

Investigate to Determine the Truth. I mentioned that I hoped that you would be honest with yourselves and honest with the Church. Now when ideas and teachings which seem to be contrary to what you have been taught all your lives are presented to you, instead of jumping to conclusions, will you be willing to be honest with the Church, with the faith of your fathers, with yourself? Will you be honest enough to really make an investigation? If people bring to you peculiar notions that you know are not taught by the Church, be honest with the Church, investigate those things before accepting them. Because they may border on the spectacular or because they happen to come from somebody who may have impressed you in an unusual way, don't take them as gilt-edged truth until you have investigated. Remember that this Church has a great history. Remember that some of the best brains that ever lived on the earth have been in this Church and upon investigation have decided that it is true. And who are we, any one of us, to throw down the result of that experience? [*Mark E. Petersen* 5]

Patient Search for Truth. The Lord God who gave us life also gave it meaning, and made all else in the universe, or brought it together and organized it. He is not in confusion, even though men sometimes are. But truth and the universe are an integrated whole. They are not conflicting segments. And sometimes the things we don't know (of which there is infinitely much) become too large in our eyes; that is, we become too impatient. And sometimes this impatience (which may properly be a part of the desire to learn, of the urge to search, but which must be moderated) may lead us to jump to quick conclusions which seem appropriate at the moment, but which time may prove to be less than satisfying, less than true. . . .

I am comforted by the fact, and I commend it to you, that with an insatiable appetite to know the answers we may also have the patience to wait for the right ones. And where there is controversy and doubt, remember there is time ahead and eternity also—and we can afford to wait. . . .

Truth is a great thing. It is a thrill to search for it, a thrill to find it. Search insatiably, and have patience where there is doubt and controversy—for the Lord God is not in confusion, and one segment of truth is not in conflict with another. If it seems to be, it is simply because we do not know enough. I commend to you patience, along with your eager searching, which I also commend to you. [*Richard L. Evans* 1]

Science and Religion. There is no conflict between true science and true religion. Science is concerned with facts and truths. Scientific men speculate and theorize in research to establish facts and truths. But until proved, they must not be accepted as the ultimate and such teachings must harmonize with *revealed* truth. Otherwise they could destroy true faith and thus bring unhappy results. [*Delbert L. Stapley* 1]

It was once thought, and still is in some places, that when a young man sets out upon a quest for academic knowledge, his faith in God would soon be destroyed. You yourselves are living proof to the contrary. It is not the search for knowledge—nor knowledge itself—that costs a man his faith. It is rather the conceit of small minds proving anew that a little knowledge can be a dangerous thing. It is intellectual pride that leads one to think he is self-sufficient in matters of mind and of spirit. Let us ever realize the vast difference that exists between discovery of truth and the Custodian of all Truth. The one is human; the Other is divine.

Religion and science have sometimes been in apparent conflict. Yet, the conflict can only be apparent, not real, for science seeks truth, and true religion is truth. There can never be conflict between revealed religion and scientific fact. That they have occupied different fields of truth is a mere detail. The gospel accepts and embraces all truth; science is slowly expanding her arms and reaching into the invisible domain, in search of truth. The two are meeting daily; science as a child; revealed religion as the mother. Truth is truth, whether labelled science or religion. All truth is consistent. There can be no conflict. [*Ezra Taft Benson* 3]

Now, I propose to present to you a phase of education in which nearly all college students are interested, and with which many have had disturbing experiences. What is the reconciliation between science and religion? Can their findings be reconciled? Can a student study science and retain his faith? I certainly have no time for an extended dissertation on these questions, even if I were capable of giving one. I am certainly not in a position to tell each student just how and when he can make such a reconciliation, but I do feel justified in assuring all students that they have a better

opportunity and a greater prospect of satisfying their thinking and their consciences on these matters in this university
[BYU] than in any others of which I have knowledge.
I give this assurance on two premises: first, that here is to
be found true religion with knowledge about God and man
and the controlling principles of life obtained from the only
source from which true religion may come—the revelations
from the Lord himself; and second, that here also is to be
found a concept of intelligence which is the foundation of
science, which likewise may authentically come from one
source only—the revelations of the Lord.

Under the revelations the province and domain of
science is far more easily understood. Its apparent incom-
patibility with religious truths is dissolved. The methods
of approach to religion and science are sufficiently differ-
entiated to justify the processes of research with no dim-
inution of faith. The virtues of study, humility and prayer
find their place in both approaches. The things of God are
understood by the spirit of God, the things of man by the
spirit of man. [*Stephen L Richards* 3]

I am happy to belong to a church, in which no man
has ever warned me against the inquiry of the mind, and
for that I am grateful. I am happy in the thought that I
belong to an institution which, in its Thirteenth Article of
Faith, bids me to go out and search the wide world over for
the truths that have come to mark civilization. I come to
you with a conviction, and I pass it on to you as I hurry by:
do not ever let yourselves get disturbed that there may be
conflict as between revealed religions and the search of
science. One day we shall complete the search. And because
we believe in continued revelation, one day there will be
brought together in complete harmony the full findings of
truth in science and the full findings of truth as revealed
by God, and when the story is written fully, we shall discover that they join hands together as great allies and not
as enemies. [*Adam S. Bennion* 2]

United Order

The United Order was tried in a small way in Kirtland, Ohio, as you may know. The real test came in Independence, Missouri, where it was set up as the way of life—the Lord's way of life. But it failed, and it failed in a short period of time. It failed because, as it was practiced, it did not stimulate and make possible the efforts of each individual according to his ability. Because of the pressures of the time the property was not deeded, and thus people did not own their own land. Most of those who joined the program were more interested in the second principle, to each according to need, not recognizing that this followed only as a blessing when people give and work according to their ability. [*William F. Edwards*]

Wisdom

Ability to See. I think that I am old enough to have learned that we are the results of the experiences of life, and I am grateful for the choice and lovely experiences that have come into my life, for the men and women that have touched that living and those experiences and have helped to interpret them for me.

Let me try to illustrate what I am talking about. The other Sunday down in Tucson, Arizona, I attended Sunday School at the Institute. A young lady stood up and gave a splendid talk entitled, "Finding God or Knowing God," and there is a vast difference. As part of her talk she told of visiting the Grand Canyon and of how greatly she was impressed with the handiwork of the Almighty, with the glory and the beauty of it all. It made a definite impression in her life. I could not help but think of a story . . . of a boy scout enroute to the jamboree. He stopped at that same Grand Canyon, looked at the same sight, and wrote his impression on a postcard which he sent to his mother in which he said, "Today, I spit a mile." They were both looking at the same thing. They did not see the same thing. And that is what is important. [*Elbert R. Curtis*]

Vision. Most of us are like children, dropping one thing each time something new is offered. We often trade our future happiness for some present pleasure. There is an optical illusion in life which makes everything in the present look large and important and everything in the future look small and unimportant. Some trinket today may seem of greater worth than mansions in heaven fifty years in the future. Vision is to understand now, how things will look when we stand at the gates of eternity and look back. [*Sterling W. Sill 2*]

Word of Wisdom

Maintaining Standards. In that year (1939) another young man just thirty-nine years of age came to Washington. He came there at the request of the National Council of Farmer Co-operatives, which represents nearly all of the farmer co-operatives in this country. At one time it represented, I recall, farm co-operatives in 98 percent of all the country. This young man came there to be interviewed for the top position—Executive Secretary of that organization. He came without having made any application; he had been sought. He appeared before the Board of Trustees of that great national organization. And after asking a number of other questions, the chairman of that committee, who was a distinguished judge from Pennsylvania by the name of John D. Miller, turned to him and asked him if he would accept the position of Executive Secretary of that organization.

This young man, Ezra Taft Benson, then president of the Boise Stake, told them that he did not think that he would accept; that he had found that when you are the top executive of many of these organizations in Washington, you are supposed to do a lot of lobbying; that he had found that almost inherent in the situation that you do a lot of entertaining, including the giving of cocktail parties; and that he was not going to accept any job in which he would be criticized if he didn't do that because he never intended to do it.

Thereupon, Judge Miller, the white-haired venerable

leader, turned to him and said, "Mr. Benson, that's why we've selected you. We know you're a Mormon. We know your standards. We know that you will keep those standards and we don't want the lobbying activities of this organization carried on in the way that they are generally carried on. And if you come here you won't have to do that. And not only that, we hope you won't do it."

Under those conditions, Elder Benson changed his mind and accepted the position as top executive of this national organization. [*Ezra Taft Benson* 1—*statement about Elder Benson by President Ernest L. Wilkinson*]

People Want You to Be Different. Another of my experiences I would like to tell you. Often numbers of our Church members say to me, "Aren't you exposed to very many temptations? Why the lives people live when they travel on business are well known. How do you manage not to have to be part of it? When you go to parties and there is drinking, don't they want you to drink? Don't they want you to smoke?" And I have thought, "How can I get it over to the Mormon youngsters *your outside friends prefer* that you do not smoke! They prefer that you do not drink! They are honored to know you when you do not."

That is really true, and I have proved it so many times! Sometimes people I have been with expect me to disapprove of them when they have been drinking. But I say to them, "I don't mind what you do. You are not a Mormon. It is what I do that matters to me." So they are at ease, and do not mind that I am different. In fact, when they introduce me they often say, "This is Rose Marie Reid. She doesn't drink, she doesn't smoke, she's a Mormon, and she is likely to convert you if you are not careful." [*Rose Marie Reid*]

Business Pressures. One wonderful thing that happened when we were just starting in the United States and we needed so much advertising, believe me we needed a budget a hundred times larger than we had. We were worrying about how to stretch our dollars. I was commuting between here [the United States] and Vancouver, and this day I was in Canada when Mr. Kessler phoned me and said, "Rose Marie, a very large company wants to use you in its advertising. They want to know when you will be back in New York so that you can be photographed in full color. They also want to show some of your suits. The ad will be on the backs of all the prominent magazines in America. They will be on billboards, newspapers—everywhere! It will amount to about $250,000 in free advertising for us and they want to know when you will be back in New York for the photographs."

And I said, "Oh Jack, tell them I will go *any time* for that."

He said, "There is only one hitch in it; you have to say that you smoke cigarettes."

I said, "Oh, my goodness! Well ask if I can say .... must be the best because my partner smokes them."

He said, "No, the slogan is: 'Experience is the best teacher,' and so they want you, and *you* have to say that."

And I said, "Well Jack, you know the answer. I couldn't possibly."

He said, "Don't answer now, I will call you tomorrow. You think about it."

Then the most wonderful thing happened. He said, "Rose Marie, Nina and I talked this over, and we would have been afraid for the future of this business if you had said 'Yes.' It will be made up to us many times. Don't you even give it another thought." [*Rose Marie Reid*]

Importance of Exemplary Living. President Bringhurst of the Swiss Temple was once on an assignment of the First Presidency in Texas. As he boarded a very large plane at one of the airports, he became aware that it was the maiden flight of that plane. Top officials of the company were on board. They had come along for a big celebration. Instead of expressing their gratitude for their progress by offering up a prayer to the Lord, they were paying their respects to the baser instincts of men by seeing how much champagne they could imbibe. A charming stewardess offered some to President Bringhurst, and he refused. She offered it the second time telling him it would be a bad omen on the maiden voyage if he didn't join in the conviviality. He did not respond. She tried the third time by asking if he wouldn't just be sociable with her—but again failed. Thereafter the officers of the company interceded—and accused him of not being a "he" man. But President Bringhurst persisted in his refusal.

As the plane was about to land, a second stewardess took a seat beside him. He expected she would exert further pressure, but instead she saluted him as "Brother Bringhurst."

He inquired, "How do you know me?"

She answered, "Some six months ago in Walla Walla, Washington, you baptized me as a member of your Church. I am proud you did not let me down. I told the other stewardess you wouldn't drink but she and the company officers said they could get you to drink—so they took up a collection to induce the other stewardess to persuade you to do so. Now that she failed she has turned the collection over to me and I am giving it to you for our missionary work." [*Ernest L. Wilkinson* 1]

. . . Dr. Frank West tells the story of going down to Texas on Church business, and he said that nothing is more monotonous than to drive over those long Texas roads on a hot afternoon. He was doing that, and he became drowsy. He thought, the first lunch counter I come to I will stop and get a cup of coffee. Now I could take a "no-doz" tablet, he reasoned, but I think the coffee will be less harmful. He came to a lunch stand, went in, sat down, and the young lady came to get his order. He said, "I will have a cheese sandwich and a glass of milk." When he was halfway through he thought, "How foolish; I came in to get a cup of coffee; well, I am glad I didn't. The milk has refreshed me; I can drive on."

When he finished the sandwich and the milk, the young lady walked up and said, "What will you have for dessert, Brother West?"

"Brother West? How did you know me?"

"You used to be my Sunday School teacher in Logan." [*A. Walter Stevenson*]

Liquor the Master.   I have a picture of a man who was once in prison. I have in my office the records of those men in prison. On those records is only the evil these men have done—everything they have done that is evil from the time they were born, almost, until they were imprisoned. There is nothing good on this record. This man's record: Forty-seven years of age, drunkard, wouldn't work, spent every cent he earned for whiskey; he had six children; his wife had to work to take care of the family. On one job when the man he was working for stepped out of the room, he picked up the adding machine and started downstairs to see if he could sell it to get some more whiskey. He was arrested and put in prison. Two years in prison! He was out on parole for two years. Toward the end of that time he got drunk again and was put back in the county jail to await return to prison for violating his parole. There one Sunday afternoon he hung himself on his cell door with his belt. And you say, "What a character!"

That was his record. That wasn't the man I knew. I met this man in prison. As I would walk down that long corridor before coming into the prison proper, there would be a little fellow, a smile on his face, and he would say, "Ray, I wrote you another poem today." Nearly every Sunday he would write a poem for me, and I compiled them in a little booklet. I want to read one or two of those poems to you this morning. I put on the front of the booklet, "Men should be judged by the desires of their hearts." To me this man lived inside these pages. He wrote one about his home. You can imagine what kind of a home he had, but he wrote:

Our home is but a shabby shack
Upon a city street,
A drooping rose in front and back,
A broken lovers' seat.

But there is a laughter in the air,
Children around the door
An old hound dog that loved them too—
Who could ask for more?

And there is peace and quiet within,
We things in common share:
Faith in God, boundless love
Of those who really care.

My blue-eyed angel, sweetheart mine,
Mother on my throne,
"Your love and grace enchant this place,
And make it home sweet home."

Our home is but a shabby shack
Upon a city street,
A drooping rose in front and back,
A broken lovers' seat.

Three years ago just before Thanksgiving, he wrote this. Two years ago just before Thanksgiving, to his boys and girls, I read it at his funeral service, he wrote:

On this Thanksgiving day, as you think of your dad,
Just remember the good and forget the bad.
When you were tiny and your prayers were said,
It wasn't always mother who tucked you in bed.

When you quarreled with your playmates
And bitterly cried,
Wasn't your old man the guy on your side?

You wished to step out,
But your chances were slim,
And your mother would say,
"Well, go and ask him."

Your dad is getting gray,
And he isn't so spry,
But he thinks of his kids
As each day goes by;

You will find every day
That it's human to err;
To forgive is divine,
If you really care.

So on this Thanksgiving Day,
Please think of your dad,
Just remember the good,
Forget the bad.

[*Ray F. Smith*]

Work

Learn to work hard. Learn to think clearly. Learn to observe carefully. Learn to observe things for yourself. [*George Albert Smith, Jr.*]

Importance of Work.   I see no evidence that the Lord God intended that any of us should live effortlessly. All the evidence is to the contrary, including his commandments. There is a striking illustration of what happens to men when things are too easy for them in the safety records of one of the best engineered pieces of highway in the world—one in which all intersections have been eliminated, and virtually all distractions also, and where the going is about as smooth as the going could be. One would think that it would have a well nigh perfect safety record. Quite to the contrary, there have been many major accidents, including fatal accidents. The explanation of some engineers is that it is too easy: that it is so easy to drive that it is almost effortless, and has a hypnotic effect. A driver loses his sense of responsibility in some degree.

I think it isn't too difficult to carry over the implications of this illustration in life. Some things could be too easy. Some of the difficulties of learning, of doing, of living, whether we like them or not at the moment, have their purpose and are for our good, and, indeed, we should not grow or develop without them. We should not want to drive through life in a hypnotic state. And more of the crashes and disappointments might well come to us (as they have been demonstrated to do in a physical sense) on a highway that is too easy to drive. [*Richard L. Evans* 1]

A Lazy People? The fallacy of American logic, I am afraid, is that we have finally concluded that the most wonderful experiences of life—the experience of achieving, the experience of acquiring excellence in some area of performance, the experience of going out and doing battle and conquering and of thereby developing the great God-given talents within us—can be had vicariously. And that, I think, should give all serious-minded men cause for deep concern. [*David S. King*]

Abilities Incorporated. It is the story of a man who was born without a chance. These crutches figure in the story. They were brought to me in the Waldorf Astoria by a man who was born without legs. Two little twisted feet were attached to his abdomen. He spent four agonizing years in a hospital where doctors worked to adjust those little feet to make a base upon which to shuffle along.

As time went on, he suffered all the indignities, cruelties and tortures which only children and human beings know how to inflict upon the unfortunate.

One day, his little heart filled with anguish, he came to his mother and asked, "Mother, why was I born this way?" The mother gathered him into her arms, held him close and she looked tenderly into his pitiful little face and said, "Henry, each year it seems that so many little crippled children must be born into the world and we like to think that before you came, Heavenly Father looked over the world of parents and decided that the Viscardi's would be a good home for you. My son, we are so grateful that you came to live with us. *We want you! We need you!! We love you!!!*" From that day on, armed with the security of that great mother love, he could face the world and conquer.

He went through schools and colleges at the head of his class and became an executive in a large corporation on the east coast where he was given the challenge to do something for the handicapped. With eight thousand dollars borrowed money he set up shop in an abandoned garage where two and a half years later he established a modern manufacturing plant, paid off his indebtedness, employed two hundred full-time workers—all handicapped—and was sending out thousands of dollars worth of vital and technical material, all 100 percent inspected and approved, to various parts of our nation.

This plant had the lowest rate of absenteeism in all America. About two years ago when storms, snows and blizzards almost closed down some of the eastern plants, only four of his people failed to show up for work and that was because of physical inability to reach the plant. Some of them came on crutches, some in wheelchairs, others crawled on hands and knees as much as two blocks through sleet and ice and snow, to reach their work. They have no grief with strikes. They don't want pity. They want work and independence through self-effort.

More acreage has now been purchased where a new plant will soon be built. Here men and women (all handicapped) from America and other countries will be trained to do for other areas that which he has done for New York.

Formerly he stood three feet eight inches. He now stands five feet eight inches on his newly acquired orthopedic legs. He is handsome, radiant, dynamic and purposeful. He has a beautiful wife and four lovely, perfect children. He personally wheeled me through his plant which they proudly called "Abilities Incorporated."

This point is this—the world is now knocking at the door of the man who was born without a chance, but because of the understanding love of an angel mother and devoted father, he dared, he worked, he won. "Love never faileth." [*Lavina Fugal*]

Be a Doer.   I should like to give you one example of many observations I have made. When I was Minister of Mines there was a young man in the accounts division who seemed most anxious and willing to do his job well. He was gradually moved up to the responsible position of chief accountant. One day I asked him if he could prepare some information for me to use the next day in the legislature. He said, "It will take a bit of doing, but we shall do our best." The next morning when I arrived at my office he was waiting for me with the material. I asked how he had been able to prepare so much in such a short time. He answered, "Oh, we knew it was important, so we stayed here and did it last night." I found that he and three others had worked all night until six a.m. to complete the job. Not long after that he became assistant deputy, and later deputy minister of the department. This was because he was not afraid of work and was determined to be of service. I am very well acquainted with another man who complains bitterly every time he is required to do just a little more than his regular job. He is still at the same job where he was years ago.

Be a doer, not a leaner. Accept responsibility. No one finds joy or satisfaction in trying to get out of work or in doing a job poorly. Joy is in accomplishment, not in drifting [*Neldon E. Tanner*]

Attitude and Work. . . . it is essential to your success and happiness that you love your work and do it the very best you can and that you make the most of yourself, having confidence in your abilities and that you accept your limitations without complaint, envy or self-pity.

I well remember an old gardener who kept the grounds and supplied the plants for the different government buildings. His pride and joy was in making those grounds as attractive and as beautiful as possible, a place where people would enjoy being. He would supply the chief offices with lovely plants which he would tend and nurture the best he knew how, always adding to the brightness and pleasantness of the office and the people in it. He enjoyed telling people how to raise and care for different plants; he was willing to help his co-workers in any way he could. No man in the government nor in its service was happier in his work or more popular or better respected than he. It matters not what honorable profession or occupation you follow, it is the attitude you assume and the way you do your work that counts. [*Neldon E. Tanner*]

INDEX

Achievement, despite adversity, 5-6, 194-195;
  satisfaction comes from, 194.
Adam, fall of, 1.
Adversity, overcoming of, 5-6, 194-195.
Angels, ministering, Aaronic Priesthood and, 138.
Anti-intellectualism, movement towards, 44-45.
Appreciation, sadness for not expressing until too late, 30-31.
Atonement, importance of, 1;
  Jesus Christ and, 1;
  repentance and, 1;
  understanding of, 1;
  based upon two truths, 1;
  relationship of fall to, 1-2.
Authority, right to challenge, 45;
  self-confidence versus, 45-46.

Baptism, peace and joy brought by, 114;
  Aaronic Priesthood and, 138.
Beginnings, importance of, 144.
Benson, Ezra Taft, call to be Secretary of Agriculture, 8-12;
  chosen as Executive Secretary of National Council of Farmer Cooperatives, 186.
Bishop, obligation to Aaronic Priesthood, 139-141.
Blessings, obtained by obedience, 118.
Blind, healing of, 158.
Bodies, importance of, 136.
Brigham Young University, role of in Church education, 41-43;
  position of among universities, 41;
  educational concept at, 41;
  objectives of, 41-42, 42-43, 43;
  purpose of, 42;
  the Lord's university, 43-44;
  attitude toward secular learning at, 44;
  problem of science and religion and, 181-182;

Church standards at, 102-103.
Callis, Charles A., baptism of, 112.
Character, potential development of, 3;
  influence of thought upon, 3-4;
  depth of, 4;
  influence of subconscious mind upon, 4;
  breadth of, 4;
  maturity and, 4;

principle and, 4-5;
  honesty and, 81.
Chastity, importance of, 15-16, 74-75;
  results of disregard of, 16-20.
Child, leads father to Church activity, 139-141.
Chinese, custom of, 3-4.
Church, objectives of, 138;
  be honest with, 179-180.
Citizenship, individual responsibility for, 8;
  moral principles and, 8;
  taught at BYU, 43.
Clean living, see Moral living.
Complacency, freedom and, 61.
Confusion, the truth and, 180.
Conflict, within a religious person, 45-46;
  none between science and religion, 180-181.
Constitution, divine approval of, 68; threats to, 68-69.
Controversy, a healthy thing, 176-177.
Conviction, open mind versus, 45-46.
Council in Heaven, two plans presented in, 55.
Courtship, eternal, 20-21;
  inadequate, 26-27.
  (See Dates and Marriage.)
Cowley, Matthew, experience while father could not exercise priesthood, 76-80.
Creation, an on-going process, 135-136.
Culture, example of life without, 38-39;
  a necessity, 39.

Dances, conduct at, 101.
Dare to do, 6-7.
Dates, conduct on, 14-15;
  influence of home governs, 15.
Dead, raising the, 162.
Death, two kinds of, 1, 29;
  second, 29;
  part of eternal plan, 30;
  preparing for, 30;
  failure to express appreciation before, 30-31;
  as viewed by excommunicant, 106-107;
  pioneer story of, 122-124;
  practices in New Zealand concerning, 161-162.
Desires, influence of, 3-4.
Discipline, love and, 145-146.

Dowling, Michael J., story of, 5-6.
Drunkenness, tragedy of, 190-192.

Education, determination to obtain, 32;
    "snap" courses, 32-33;
    no easy road to, 32-33, 35;
    purpose of, 34, 35;
    scientific method of, 34;
    a necessity, 35;
    rises above gaining a living, 38-39;
    a preparation for life, 35;
    results of Church, 39-41;
    role of BYU in Church, 41-43;
    concept at BYU, 41;
    importance of among Latter-day
        Saints, 42;
    movement to impede, 44-45;
    problem of science and religion in,
        181-182;
    freedom and, 62.
    (See Teacher.)
Education, liberal, path to wisdom, 37-
    38;
    importance of, 38.
Effort, necessary to gain knowledge, 34.
Eisenhower, Dwight, spiritual attitude
    of, 11-12.
Exaltation, progress toward, 30;
Example, importance of living an, 100-
    102, 109, 188-189, 189-190;
    power of, 102-103.
Excommunication, sorrow because of,
    104-107.
Faith, rationalizing and, 49;
    blind, 26-27;
    challenge of science to, 181-182;
    importance of, 49;
    a simple, 49;
    purpose of, 49-50;
    sight and, 49, 50, 51;
    knowledge and, 50;
    limitations of, 50, 51;
    naive, 51;
    works necessary with, 52-53;
    living for, 53;
    reason and, 52-53;
    of pioneers, 122-124;
    healing and, 158-163.
Fall, related to atonement, 1;
    results of, 1.
Family, importance of, 27;
    an eternal unit, 76.
Fasting and prayer, a preparation for
    giving blessings, 158-159.
Forgiveness, conditions for obtaining,
    19-20;
    our obligation to grant to others,
        145-146; 146-148.
Foresight, importance of, 184-185.

truth and, 60, 63;
    threats to, 61;
    responsibility of free men for, 61;
    complacency and, 61;
Freedom, even though in bonds, 56;
    responsibility and, 60;
    definition of, 60;
    conditions necessary for national and
        individual, 62;
    obedience and, 62;
    law and, 62, 96, 119;
    education and, 62;
    foreign "isms" and, 62-63;
    road to, 63;
    government - supported security and,
        63-64, 69-70;
    government and, 69-70, 70-71;
    a gift of God, 69-70.
Free Agency, Council in Heaven and,
    55;
    growth through, 55;
    a great gift, 56;
    choice of two ways, 56;
    responsibility in, 58-59.

Gambling, dangers of, 65.
God, personality of, 67;
    communist attitude toward, 129.
Godhead, importance of knowledge of,
    66;
    understanding of, 66-67.
Godhood, ultimate goal of man, 66.
Gospel, teaching in the home, 76-80;
    greatest message in the world, 93-94;
    results of living the commandments
        of, 97-98;
    fullness of, 137.
Government, principle and, 68;
    concentration of power in, 68-69, 70-
        71;
    tests of services of, 69-70;
    freedom and, 69-70.
Grand Canyon, two impressions of,
    184.
Gratitude, elements of, 72;
    depth of, 72-73.

Habits, importance of beginnings, 144.
Handicap, overcoming of, 5-6, 194-195.
Happiness, result of obedience, 119.
Hawaii, story of school in, 36-37.
Healing, 158-163;
    of the blind, 159;
    of polio, 159-161;
    of the lame, 163.
Holy Ghost, leads to a knowledge of the
    things of God, 94.
Home, importance of, 74;
    as a missionary, 75-76;

importance of gospel teaching in, 76-80.
Honesty, fundamental principle of the gospel, 81.
Hypocrisy, results of, 108-109.

Ignorance, products of, 178.
Immortality, eternal life and, 48.
Inspiration, a type of revelation, 150.
Intelligence, eternal nature of, 135-136.

Jesus Christ, atonement and, 1-2;
literal Son of God, 82;
role in Council in Heaven, 55;
principle and, 68;
complete concept of, 82;
as Redeemer, 82-83;
as God, 83;
suffering of, 83;
power of teachings, 83, 84;
importance of knowing, 84-86;
as a story teller, 84-85;
thirteen statements about, 84-86;
as a public speaker, 85;
unjust trial of, 86-87;
Old Testament prophecies of, 86-87.
Joy, real meaning of, 95.

Knowledge, power of in Church, 35;
acquisition of, 41;
acquired through education, 42;
gained by effort, 44;
faith and, 50;
of Godhead, 66;
loss of faith and, 181.

Law, limitations of, 96;
twofold purpose of, 96;
selfishness versus, 96;
eternal nature of, 118;
freedom and, obedience to, 119.
Laws, obeying God's, 56-57;
obedience to, 118.
Learning, two sources of, 43;
attitude toward secular, 44;
attitude toward laws of, 44;
must work to gain, 44;
advancement of, 176.
Liberty, see Freedom.
Life, purpose of, 51, 57;
two forces in, 56;
depth of religious, 97.
Life, eternal, available to all, 47;
based on personal progress, 47;
role of earth life in, 47-48, 136;
immortality and, 48;
temple work and, 166.
Living our religion, in the business world, 98;

importance of, 100-102;
only on Sunday, 103.
Love, discipline and, 145-146;
child teaches lesson in, 146;
feeling of security from, 194;
of a mother, 194-195.

Man, sees beyond reason, 35.
Maeser, Karl G., gift of tongues and 164-165.
Marriage, beginning of happy, 14;
eternal, 21, 74-75;
living worthy of eternal, 21-23;
danger of to non-members, 23-26;
within the Church, 23;
qualities to look for mate in, 25;
mature attitude toward, 26-27;
Christ's counsel on, 27;
children and, 27-28;
BYU and, 28;
importance of temple, 78-79;
attitude of some non-LDS toward eternal, 166-167.
Maturity, breadth of, 4.
McKay, David O., story about, 6-7.
Mercy, repentance the price for, 144.
Miracles, healing, 158-163;
raising the dead, 162;
gift of tongues, 163-165.
Mission field, baptismal services in, 114.
Missionary, the home as, 75-76;
everyone a, 111.
Missionary work, divisions of, 111;
importance on one soul, 112;
industry needed in, 112-113;
rewards of, 113, 114;
in Brazil, 113-114;
one obligation of Aaronic Priesthood, 139.
Money, true worth of, 5.
Moral Living, challenge to, 115.
Morality, single standard of, 15-16;
personal responsibility for, 115-116.

Necking, See Petting.
Needs, social, list of, 4.

Obedience, discipline versus, 117;
love and, 117, 117-118;
fear and, 117;
rewards of, 56, 118, 119;
liberty obtained by, 119;
does not guarantee escape from trials, 119;
personal responsibility for intelligent, 119-120.
Old Testament, prophecies of Jesus Christ, 86-87.
Open mind, conviction versus, 45-46.

Ordinances, characteristics of, 137-138;
  sacrifice and sacrament, 155-156;
  first principles and, 179.

Patience, in search for truth, 180.
Patriarch, mission of, 121.
Patriarchal blessings, one purpose of,
  121;
  from the Lord, 121.
Peace of mind, result of obedience,
  117-118, 119.
Persons, God no respecter of, 118.
Petting, danger of, 16-20.
Pioneers, story of faith of, 122-124.
Polio, boy healed of, 159-161.
Politics, Church attitude toward, 9-10.
Potential, of human character, 3;
  some people lost to their, 146.
Pray, when to, 132-134.
Prayer, in Matthew Cowley's home, 77-
  78;
  as viewed by excommunicant, 105-
  106;
  role in restoration of gospel, 126;
  importance of, 126-127;
  secret, 126;
  great men and, 127;
  source of strength, 126-127;
  God will answer, 127-128, 139;
  preparation for, 128-129;
  God answers a little girl's, 129-130;
  of a man in prison, 130-132;
  answer from wrong source, 153-154.
Pre-existence, reasonableness of, 135;
  of all mankind, 135;
  scriptures teach, 135.
Principle, character and, 4-5;
  citizenship and, 8;
  government and, 68;
  temptation to abandon, 98;
  double standard of, 103.
Priesthood, keys of, 137;
  ordinances and, 137-138;
  one function of, 138;
  powers of Aaronic, 138;
  Senior Aaronic, 138-139;
  reproving with sharpness, 141-142.
Prison, Utah State, stories from, 107-
  110, 130-132, 146-148, 190-192.
Prophecy, Holy Ghost guides to understanding of, 149.
Prophet, characteristics of, 91-93;
  world's need for, 94.
Purity, See Chastity.

Radio, reception compared to revelation,
  153-154.
Rationalizing, faith versus, 49.
Reason, faith and, 53-54.

Redeemer, See Jesus Christ.
Religion, science and, 180-182;
  characterized by three doctrines, 53;
  practical, 125.
Repentance, limitations of, 143;
  efficacy of atonement dependent
  upon, 1;
  Aaronic Priesthood and, 138;
  justice and, 144;
  retracing steps, 144.
Resurrection, Alma's discussion of, 133-
  134.
Responsibility, freedom and, 60;
  for citizenship, 8;
  free agency and, 58-59;
  free men and, 61;
  for intelligent obedience, 119-120.
Revelation, logical support for continuous, 89-91;
  present in the Church today, 149;
  inspiration a type of, 150;
  example of a child receiving, 150-151;
  example of members in New Zealand
  receiving, 151;
  righteous prepared to receive, 152-154;
  compared to radio reception, 153-154;
  accepting, 178.
Righteousness, satisfying nature of, 116;
  evil opposition to, 130-131;
  ordinances and, 137-138.

Sacrament, definition of, 155-156.
Sacrifice, purpose of, 155.
Satan, role in Council in Heaven. 55.
Savior, See Jesus Christ.
Science and religion, 180-182.
Scientific method, in education, 34.
Service, to God and men, 157.
Service Organizations, obligation of
  Church members to serve in, 12-13.
Servicemen, religious experience of, 39-
  41.
Sin, two kinds of, 143;
  to be repentantly remembered, 144.
Smith Joseph, bearing testimony of,
  79-80;
  importance of in gospel plan, 88;
  Elder Hugh B. Brown's "profile" of,
  88-94;
  testimony of from Holy Ghost, 94;
  prayer and, 126.
Society, role of home in, 74.
Son of God, See Jesus Christ.
Soul, importance of one, 112.
Spencer, Orson, story of, 122-124.
Spirit, eternal nature of, 135-136.
Spiritual gifts, healing, 158-163;
  raising the dead, 162;
  gift of tongues, 163-165.

Standards, Church, recognition of, 9;
    results of maintaining, 21-23;
    result of disregarding, 104;
    and testimony, 168;
    business success and, 99.
Subconscious mind, influence upon
    character, 3;
    power of, 3.
Success, Church standards and, 99.

Teachings, power of Christ's, 83, 84.
Teachers, responsibility of religious, 35;
    qualities of great, 36;
    lasting influence of great, 36-37.
Temptations, purpose of, 48.
Temples, importance of, 166.
Temple work, a missionary, 166;
    a scriptural doctrine, 167.
Ten Commandments, fundamental na-
    ture of, 57.
Testimony, of Joseph Smith, 79-80, 94;
    effect of bearing, 150;
    maintaining Church standards and,
    168;
    steps necessary to obtain, 168;
    learning of men and, 168;
    Holy Ghost leads to, 168;
    a support in Church work, 168-170;
    can come at any age, 170-171;
    a child leads to, 170-171;
    of Elder Marion D. Hanks, 172-173;
    of Elder Matthew Cowley, 173;
    of Elder Mark E. Petersen, 173-174.
Thanks, expression to God, 40.
Thought, influence upon character, 3-4.
Tithing, temptation not to pay, 98;
    a testimony of, 175.
Tobacco, resisting use of, 187-188.
Tolerance, of Church, 178.
Tongues, gift of, David O. McKay in
    New Zealand, 163-164;
    interpretation of, 163-164;
    Karl G. Maeser and, 164-165.
Truth, as taught at BYU, 41;
    importance of, 176;
    free inquiry into, 176;
    Unity of thought and, 176-177;
    individual responsibility to discover,
    177;

mission of Church and, 177;
    narrowness of, 177-178;
    learning of solves problems, 178;
    arbitrariness of, 178-179;
    Holy Ghost leads to, 179;
    means of testing, 179;
    learning of men and, 179-180, 181;
    search for, 180;
    gospel embraces all, 181.
    See Learning.
Unhappiness, disregard of law brings,
    118.
United Order, reasons for failure of,
    183.
University, purpose of university life,
    34;
    purpose of a, 44.

Virtue, See Chastity.
Vision, first, fundamental truths re-
    vealed in, 93-94.

Ward teachers, good performed by, 141.
Warning, given by excommunicated
    member, 106-107.
Waste, greatest in world, 3.
Wisdom, source of good ideas, 37-38;
    definition of, 41;
    experience and, 184.
Wisdom, Word of, recognition for liv-
    ing, 186;
    business success and, 187;
    non-members expect members to ob-
    serve, 187-188;
    resisting pressure to disregard, 188-
    189;
    tragedy because of disregarding of,
    190-192.
Women, National Council, Relief So-
    ciety membership in, 12-13.
Work, necessary to achieve anything
    worth while, 32-33;
    necessary to gain knowledge, 34, 44;
    some purposes of, 193;
    American tendency to avoid, 194;
    rewards from diligent, 195-196;
    attitude toward, 196.

AUTHOR INDEX

Allen, Mark K., 4, 44.

Bennett, Archibald F., 166.
Bennion, Adam S., 99, 182.
Bennion, Lowell L., 26-27, 50, 51, 103.
Benson, Ezra Taft, 8-12, 42-43, 62-63, 69-70, 74-75, 126-127, 181, 186-187.
Berrett, William E., 62, 63.
Brown, Hugh B., 39-41, 56-57, 66-67, 88-94, 118, 119, 135-136.
Buehner, Carl W., 138-139, 139-141.

Christensen, Parley A., 72-73.
Christiansen, ElRay L., 55-56, 58, 76, 117, 118, 135.
Clark, Bruce B., 164-165.
Clark, J. Reuben, Jr., 29, 32-33, 49, 55, 68, 82-83, 143.
Cowley, Matthew, 5-6, 76-80, 117-118, 151-152, 158-163, 173.
Curtis, Elbert R., 184.

deJong, Gerrit, Jr., 38-39.
DeMille, Cecil B., 57, 96, 111.
Dixon, Henry Aldous, 36, 118.

Edwards, William F., 47, 183.
Evans, Richard L., 58-59, 144, 180, 193-194.

Fugal, Lavina, 43-44, 194-195.

Glade, Earl J., 95.

Hanks, Marion D., 57, 60, 62, 119, 132-134, 144, 145-146, 157, 170-171, 172-173, 178.

Kimball, Spencer W., 6-20, 47-48, 58, 136.

King, David S., 194.
Kirkham, Oscar A., 36-37.

Lee, Harold B., 21-23, 30-31, 52-53, 75-76, 100-102, 104-107, 112, 119-120, 129-130, 149, 150-151, 152-154, 175.
Longden, John, 125.

McConkie, Bruce R., 1-2, 137-138.
McKay, David O., 14-15, 15-16, 20-21, 27-28, 34, 35, 53-54, 83, 97-98, 163-164.
McKay, Thomas E., 6-7.
McKinlay, Lynn A., 97, 116.
Mendenhall, Wendell, 171-172.
Morgan, Nicholas G., Sr., 122-124.
Morris, George Q., 3, 176, 177-178, 178-179.
Moyle, Henry D., 34, 35, 37-38, 41, 49, 66, 67, 70-71, 96, 111, 144, 176-177.

Nash, Jay B., 61.
Nibley, Preston, 88, 126.
Nicholes, Henry J., 34.

Petersen, Mark E., 42, 53, 81, 115-116, 173-174, 178, 179-180.

Reid, Rose Marie, 99, 187-188.
Richards, LeGrand, 23-24, 24-26, 121, 149, 166-167, 168-170.
Richards, Stephen L, 21, 23, 28, 35, 41-42, 65, 112-113, 113-114, 115, 138, 141-142, 181-182.
Romney, Marion G., 43, 56, 63-64, 150, 157, 168, 179.

Sill, Sterling W., 3, 4, 5, 50, 184-185.

Smith, George Albert, Jr., 44-45, 45-46, 193.

Smith, Joseph Fielding, 30, 48, 49-50, 51, 56, 83, 135.

Smith, Milan D., 5, 98, 168.

Smith, Ray F., 107-110, 130-132, 146-148, 190-192.

Sonne, Alma, 84-86.

Spafford, Belle S., 12-13, 102-103.

Stapley, Delbert L., 83, 155-156, 180-181.

Stevenson, A. Walter, 189-190.

Tanner, Neldon E., 119, 196-197.

Taylor, Harvey L., 8, 61.

Wilkinson, Ernest L., 32, 68-69, 86-87, 186-187, 188-189.

Wirthlin, Joseph L., 138, 139.

Young, S. Dilworth, 127-128, 128-129.